Stop Smoking *and Vaping* Now!

T0049791

OTHER BOOKS BY
Karen Casey

Stop Smoking and Vaping Now!

How to Recover
from Nicotine Addiction

Karen Casey

CORAL GABLES, FL

For permission requests, please contact the publisher at:
Mango Publishing Group
2850 S Douglas Road, 2nd Floor
Coral Gables, FL 33134 USA
info@mango.bz

For special orders, quantity sales, course adoptions and corporate sales, please email the publisher at sales@mango.bz. For trade and wholesale sales, please contact Ingram Publisher Services at customer.service@ingramcontent.com or +1.800.509.4887.

Stop Smoking and Vaping Now!: How to Recover from Nicotine Addiction

Library of Congress Cataloging-in-Publication number: 2023949530
ISBN: (pb) 978-1-68481-484-8 (e) 978-1-68481-485-5
BISAC: SEL026010, SELF-HELP / Substance Abuse & Addictions / Tobacco

Table of Contents

Part III: Meditations

What Everyone Should Know about Vaping

When I first heard about vaping from a teenager about a decade ago, I was not particularly alarmed. I had seen so many different trends come and go and had no reason to believe this would be any different.

A short period of time thereafter, my clients began to bring vapes and vaping apparatuses into our sessions. I quickly learned that each cartridge can contain an enormous amount of nicotine. And to be honest, from a teenager's perspective, all the tools that come with vaping seem pretty cool. I suspect that any of us who would've been around when vaping was introduced to the marketplace would've been drawn to it.

Most of my clients swore off vaping immediately. Then, within a period of just a few weeks, they would report that they had tried it, but only once or twice. After another few weeks, they were vaping every day. And then, within months, an awful lot of my clients were vaping all day, every day. They were absolutely addicted to nicotine.

One might think that, like so many other drugs, vaping has become the bastion of troubled or difficult kids. Our A students who are involved in extracurriculars and have groups of friends would have no need for it. But they are just as likely to become addicted to nicotine in this way as anyone else. I find all kids, especially boys and young men, to be susceptible. And it's important to note that the initial age for vaping has dropped precipitously over the years. Now, it is not uncommon to find a sixth or seventh grader who vapes regularly.

I began to find vapes, mods, and cartridges between the cushions of my couch every single week. That continues to this day.

There's another element of the vaping epidemic that's important to recognize. Kids don't just vape nicotine. They can also vape marijuana. A lot of adults are unaware of the reality that these two drugs, in large part because of the similarity of the delivery systems, have become gateways to one another. Rarely will you find a teenager or young adult who vapes nicotine and does not vape marijuana, or vice versa. Add "hitting" a vape becomes habitual and ritualistic very quickly. That is, I see kids hit vapes of all kinds unconsciously, but it adds to their addiction and potential health problems quite readily.

And speaking of health problems, an ER doctor recently sent me chest scans of a recently deceased, ninety-year-old woman who had been smoking since she was a teenager. He also sent me scans of a seventeen-year-old boy who had been vaping for about two and a half years. And the scans looked identical. My MD friend suggested that we are on the cusp of potentially severe upper respiratory and cardiovascular disease among our young people.

So, I have come to loathe the idea of vaping. These things are very cleverly designed to elude parents: they are small and nearly odorless. And further, they virtually guarantee addiction.

So, if you are a parent, or if you have influence over a young person in your life, talk to them about the dangers of vaping. Start young, and don't assume they don't know everything about it. In all likelihood, they do. Your opinion may not drive all of their behavior, but it does weigh heavily on what they do. Weigh in. Get your voice in the mix. You may be saving a child from a fixation, an addiction, or potentially a life-threatening illness.

And my strong bias is that we all do what we can to eradicate vaping from the marketplace as soon as possible.

Vaping and smoking are both bad for your overall health, but especially your lungs. And you need your lungs to breathe! Vape pens often contain ultra-fine particles that get inhaled deep into your lungs and cause damage that will get worse as the years go on. The artificial flavorings and chemical additives have been shown to cause serious damage to lungs. It is sad to see anyone of any age pick up a habit that is unhealthy, but it is downright heartbreaking to see a teenager's life cut short because they were ensnared by a candy-flavored e-cigarette. We all know that habits start pretty casually, easily, and innocently, especially a kid's attraction to a product that tastes like a sugary treat. Let's set blame aside and just urge our friends, family, and loved ones to quit both cigarettes and vaping.

Stopping a habit can be hard, but it is worth it. You are worth it.

Dr. John Duffy

PART I

Special Vaping Resources Section

Vaping of nicotine has reached epidemic levels among young people in America. Many young adults vape; but what makes this crisis even more urgent are the levels of uptake among users under the age of eighteen. Researchers at Massachusetts General Hospital found in a review of CDC data from 150,000 teens and preteens that the *average* age of first trying vaping is only thirteen years old. And far from just being a try-it-once kind of experience, daily use reported by minors who vape rose from 20 percent of them in 2020 to 25 percent in 2021—this enormous increase reflects a truly frightening trend, since nicotine vaping can function as a gateway drug that raises the likelihood of a kid who vapes going on to not only develop a long-term nicotine habit but use harder drugs.

Of course, young folks aren't the only ones employing vaping technology to consume nicotine. Here are some resources which it is hoped will serve to assist anyone, of any age, who wants to stop.

The Trouble with Vaping

These days, many of us think of nicotine vaping as something far less problematic than actually smoking or chewing tobacco; it doesn't make one's breath or clothes smell bad, and surely a little mist can't harm us the way clouds of tobacco smoke do, we may believe. What's the big issue? But the majority of the public likely isn't aware that some of these devices can deliver far more nicotine per day to users than even a three-pack-a-day cigarette habit, or that manufacturers of nicotine vaping liquid seem to go out of their way to give their products flavors designed for maximum appeal to kids, including quite young children. Vapes as a consumer offering have become so popular so quickly that regulators have struggled to keep up with issues ranging from toxic chemicals (other than nicotine) in the liquids vaporized to batteries that on occasion explode, causing fire and injury. And they are every bit as addictive as tobacco products.

What is vaping? Vaping is when a handheld electronic device is used to heat a liquid, generating a mist of aerosolized droplets, a.k.a. vapor, that users inhale into their lungs. Excluding cannabis/THC vaping, this liquid is made up of a combination of nicotine with flavoring, propylene glycol, and other additives. The inhaled aerosolized particles can inflame and irritate the lungs, in some instances leading to lung damage like scarring and narrowing of the tubes that convey air in and out of the lungs. Some of the dangerous chemicals that the liquids sold in vape cartridges have been found to contain include carcinogens like formaldehyde and acetaldehyde; lung-damaging diacetyl, diethylene glycol, and acrolein; and heavy metals such as cadmium, nickel, tin, and lead.

Vaping is becoming more and more common; as of 2020, the Centers for Disease Control report that over nine million American adults used e-cigarettes, and more than 14 percent of high school students reported current use of the devices in 2022. Research has found that teenagers who vape are more likely to begin smoking tobacco cigarettes. Just as with tobacco smoke, secondhand exposure to vaping is also becoming widespread. And in the same way that cigarettes are not safe to use during pregnancy, vaping nicotine can cause brain and lung damage and low birth weight in the developing fetus.

Although vaping nicotine is somewhat safer than smoking tobacco, in part because it exposes the user to a smaller number of dangerous chemicals than smoking, it's still bad for you. While it isn't definitively understood exactly what chemicals vapes, a.k.a. e-cigarettes, put into the lungs, according to Michael Blaha, MD, clinical research director of the John Hopkins Ciccarone Center for the Prevention of Heart Disease, "There's almost no doubt that vaping exposes you to fewer toxic chemicals than smoking traditional cigarettes." But Dr. Blaha doesn't want the public to underestimate the dangers of vaping. He explains, "Emerging data suggests links to chronic lung disease and asthma;" there are also correlations of people who both vape and smoke with having a higher probability of heart disease.

Side effects of vaping can include mouth and throat irritation, headaches, coughing, and feeling queasy. But besides the not-yet-well-understood chemicals in the liquid base, vaping allows a person to take in quantities of nicotine, sometimes well in excess of what that person could inhale if smoking cigarettes. Nicotine, besides being highly addictive, is toxic; it causes adrenaline levels to spike, which brings on rapid heartbeat, as well as elevating blood pressure. The more nicotine you take into your body, the more your risk of a heart attack rises. Although it is possible to buy extra-strength cartridges for vape pens or boost their voltage to deliver a stronger dose of nicotine, doing so maximizes the danger of an adverse health event occurring. At times, injuries and burns have also resulted from exploding batteries in vaping devices.

You might be tempted to think that vaping could be a good way for you to break your attachment to cigarettes. However, research has found that most people who tried to quit cigarettes using vaping didn't actually ever stop smoking and vaping. Nicotine is not less addictive when delivered in vapor than it is in smoke; its addictive qualities have been compared to those of crack cocaine, which are proverbially powerful.

WHAT HAPPENS WHEN YOU STOP VAPING?

- In twenty minutes, your pulse and your blood pressure come back down to normal levels.

- In three days, all nicotine will have left your body.

- After one week, withdrawal symptoms like mood swings, headaches, and increased appetite for food will be greatly decreased, if not completely gone.

Tips for Quitting Vaping

MAKE A LIST

Consider creating a list of reasons why you want to stop vaping. Revisit it daily or every so often to empower your sense of purpose as you leave behind this habitual behavior pattern.

SET A DATE TO QUIT

Do your best to find a time period when your stress levels will be at their most manageable (i.e., avoid finals week, or that big deadline push at your job!) The day *before* your quitting day, one technique to try is completely switching which hand you use to hold your vape pen or e-cigarette from the hand you habitually use. This can help to rewire the sense of reliance on familiar sensations that one experiences while vaping.

AVOID CRAVING TRIGGERS

Try to avoid triggering situations where you would normally vape, or substitute other activities where possible. If you always end up vaping around certain people, consider how you can change that dynamic.

BE READY FOR WITHDRAWAL'S SHORT-TERM SENSATIONS

Cravings are likely at first, along with headaches and possibly anxiety. Consider nicotine gum or patches to help blunt the edge at first. Your physician may be able to prescribe you medication that will ease this stage.

MAKE A PLAN

Strategize in advance how you might handle it when cravings arise. Some people who quit play a game for a minute, chew a stick of gum, or take a moment outdoors to lower stress and get past the urge to vape, which is often very brief in duration. Brainstorm some options that could work for you and take note of which ones end up working the best.

DISTRACT YOURSELF FROM TEMPTATION

Vaping urges, although sometimes intense, usually don't last that long. If you are able to distract yourself on purpose, that will help take your mind off the craving. Find something that is pleasantly distracting for you to do when an urge rears its ugly head. If you can shift your focus for even one or two minutes, chances are the urge will have passed.

GET ACTIVE

According to many experts as well as the experience of many of those trying to quit vaping, exercise is a great way to banish those cravings. TikTok influencers and YouTubers have leaned in on their running, bicycling, or even surfing, as they find that physical activity really helps turn the tables on nicotine urges.

REACH OUT FOR SUPPORT

Just as it is key when quitting cigarettes, lining up support from sympathetic friends, family members, and anyone who's been through it before themselves can be crucial to succeeding at quitting vaping. Don't hesitate to ask for this kind of support; it's not weak to do so. It truly can make the difference to you getting your power back in relation to nicotine, and then you will be able to extend an experienced helping hand to others. Joining in quitting challenges can offer a chance for fellowship with others embarking on their own stop-vaping journeys; young people who want extra support beyond their own personal network can join *This Is Quitting* by texting DITCHVAPE to 88709.

LOWER YOUR STRESS FOR SUCCESS

Some people vape because they say it helps them feel better when they're stressed out. But what if in truth, this intention tends to backfire? Research says that in reality, vaping can set up a vicious cycle of unease and cravings and may actually *intensify* anxiety and stress for many. To achieve freedom from the vaping habit, it's important to work to lower your stress—in ways that don't involve vaping. Others quitting vaped nicotine have used techniques such as meditation, talking through it with others, time in nature, and journaling to get a handle on spiking stress.

CELEBRATE YOUR PROGRESS MILESTONES

Those knowledgeable about the quitting process say there is an unexpected dividend to celebrating the steps you succeed in taking on your stop-vaping journey: Doing so can boost your ability to resist cravings, as well as lowering the stress you experience. This is true even if the step you salute is just resisting the urge to backslide for a day—it can take a lot of strength and will to accomplish that!

Try tracking your time steering clear of nicotine with an app like "Escape the Vape"—you can search on 'quit vaping' in the Play Store or in Apple apps, where you'll find many to choose from. Besides logging streaks of vape-free time, you can also add up the money you've saved and set goals, as well as tracking which milestones you've reached.

PART II

Personal Stories

My Story

The refrigerator still held its accustomed two-carton stock of cigarettes that cold December evening, just five days short of Christmas, when events mysteriously paved the way for my becoming a nonsmoker. Members of my women's A.A. group had gathered at my apartment to bring the program to me because I had been ill and was unable to get to them.

As we sat around the Christmas tree in my tiny living room, Rita began talking about her desire to quit smoking. She wanted to make that her gift to her family on that Christmas in 1976. Although the topic wasn't A.A., it was quickly apparent that it was a First Step issue. Rita was not the only one among us addicted to nicotine, and we easily saw the parallels between our struggles with alcohol and other drugs and the current struggle with cigarettes. It was true, all of our lives were controlled by our need to smoke wherever and whenever we could.

I was personally startled when I enumerated the activities that "demanded" I smoke: Driving, talking with a friend, coffee, awaiting dinner (or lunch or breakfast) in a restaurant (or at home), phone conversations, or waiting on a call, leisure bathing in a tub, the morning alarm, the many visits to the bathroom throughout the day, reading a good or a bad book for pleasure or a class, writing a letter, or a grocery list or a paper for one of my graduate courses, hurt feelings, anger, fear of abandonment, an actual or an imagined confrontation with a friend or lover, applying makeup, drying my hair, dressing for the day or evening, unwinding, preparing for bed, visiting with my Higher Power before turning out the light, cleaning house, outlining the day's activities, daydreaming, and obsessive thinking about my life or "him" or "what if"—the list was endless. I was embarrassed, but I loved smoking. I felt supportive of Rita's desire to quit, but I was quite content to carry on as usual. When friends were in need, however, I was quick to offer an ear, and sometimes unwanted advice.

The next thing I knew the words came tumbling out. But they weren't musts and shoulds; rather, they were gentle suggestions coming from some place deep within me. I heard myself speaking, but I wasn't sure who was formulating the ideas I was mouthing. "Why not make a decision to be a nonsmoker, Rita? A nonsmoker doesn't grab for her cigarettes and lighter when the phone rings. A nonsmoker can even go to the bathroom empty-handed or choose to go out for the evening purseless or matchless! A nonsmoker is free to make new choices about places to visit or activities to participate in because the first allegiance is to oneself—not to a pack of cigarettes."

I truly didn't know where my message was coming from. I was simply the messenger, a steadily puffing messenger at that. "Rita," I said, "the desire for a cigarette doesn't even cross a nonsmoker's mind. This person is free to focus on an engaging conversation, the chirping birds outside the open window, and the laughter of the children on the stairs. There is no resentment about not being able to smoke because one's identity is as a nonsmoker." I knew that, plain and simply, a nonsmoker isn't haunted by the urge to inhale the taste of tobacco.

But I was just as certain at that moment that when a smoker quit, he or she felt deprived; after all, cigarettes were friends who comforted. Cigarettes brought relief. It was no wonder I felt this way. A decade earlier, in 1966, I had tried to quit smoking. I had not, however, changed my self-perception. Although I did not smoke for six years, I was still at heart a smoker who (damn it!) didn't smoke anymore. What a relief when I finally let go of my control over it and took the plunge back into the haven of "cigaretteville." When I resumed smoking, it was with a vengeance. I was making up for lost time; it seemed almost based on anger. My consumption quickly escalated from one pack to nearly three packs daily. And never did I think of quitting again.

Yet, here I was, sharing a bit of inner wisdom with Rita about the positive aspects of smoking no more. The subtle difference between quitting a loved addiction and becoming a new personality was not lost on me, however! Moments later my speech ended, and so did that phase of my personal history. I very quietly put out my cigarette and have been a nonsmoker ever since.

I can't say that my physical body was as content with the new self-perception as was my mind. My body cried out for nicotine—loudly at times. I had heard that smoking muffled our feelings, but I didn't know how much. And I was to know a new level of rage. On not-too-rare occasions in the first three months after I had quit, all 115 pounds of me startled others as well as myself when I contemptuously screamed at unsuspecting people who wandered across my path. "What do you mean I need to tell you what weight oil to put in my car! You work here, don't you?"

But my self-talk saved me. At frequent intervals throughout each morning, each afternoon, and each evening, I took a few moments "away" from the people or task at hand to image myself as a smiling, confident nonsmoker. Fortunately, I also had a Higher Power and a Twelve Step program for strength. I was soon to discover, however, that there wasn't great support from many of my friends and acquaintances in school, at work, or at my meetings. But the strength to continue on was sustained. And with each passing day, I more firmly filled the body and the shoes of my nonsmoking self.

I detected a healthy ego response, too. It exhilarated me that I had reclaimed some personal power over my identity. I had chosen a new posture toward life; I had chosen to quit killing myself a puff at a time. The natural deduction was that I was learning to love myself—a first step to loving someone else. When the old Karen tugged at me to return to the old ways—and she did, frequently at first, but with lessening frequency as time elapsed—the new me was able to stand my ground. I was a nonsmoker and so proud of it. I was free to sit where I wanted in restaurants. My hair and clothes no longer reeked of tobacco. My apartment didn't smell like a crowded bar any longer. And after washing my car and apartment windows, I was treated to a new brightness wherever I looked. With disgust, I wiped away the yellow nicotine stains from the glass protecting the many pictures hung throughout my apartment, and my commitment to my nonsmoking life was strengthened.

Who would have thought back in 1955 that this choice would capture me in 1976? I thought smoking was sexy then. I remember all too well riding down 9th Street with Barbara in her mother's white two-door Chevy. Barbara needed both hands to steer and shift the car, so the cigarette dangled from her lips. I took one from the red-and-white box-top pack and waited for the car's cigarette lighter to pop out. My ears buzzed with the first deep draw and my head felt light. But we giggled, feeling so smart and sophisticated. My first cigarette was at a slumber party in ninth grade. But that was just girl stuff and no inhaling. This was different. This was the real thing. We had a car, a half tank of gas, and a full pack of Marlboros between us on the seat, and the evening was young.

It was understood in my family that I'd be a smoker. They were all smokers: my parents, aunts and uncles, grandparents, even my two older sisters. My dad requested that I not smoke until the age of eighteen, so I dutifully lied about it and hid my smoking; then, on my eighteenth birthday, I was given a carton of cigarettes as a present. It was my passage to adulthood.

And here I was twenty-one years later, saying, "Wait a minute, I want to make a new choice; I want to have a new identity." And so close on the heels of my turn to A.A., too. A fortunate, life-giving choice it was. The rewards have been many. I wish I could say Rita remained a nonsmoker as well. But after a few months, she returned to smoking. She was there for me during my trying times, though, and the phone lines between our homes buzzed with affirmations, cries for help, and prayers.

With confidence and full certainty, readers, I can assure you that my life as a nonsmoker is rewarding. There is no doubt that I'm healthier. My energy level is higher. I accomplish more daily because I'm not taking the accustomed cigarette breaks of years past. I play better racquetball and tennis. Hurrying up steps doesn't wind me. My hair, breath, clothes, and home no longer smell like a barroom floor. My teeth no longer have brown stains. My fingertips are a healthy pink. And I haven't lost my desire or ability to write. How certain I was that writing and cigarettes were tightly entwined. My fear was great that nonsmoking Karen would also be nonwriting Karen. However, I have four books under my belt as proof that whatever wisdom I've been blessed with to share, it didn't come from cigarettes.

What follows next are stories of other recovering smokers. There is so much each of us can gain from helping and being helped by "one who has gone before." Please read on—for the strength, the hope, and the courage to quit. Another benefit of the stories is the realization that's sure to come to you that we're all so very much alike, even though the details of our lives may differ. Giving up nicotine is a major decision. It was for each of us. but it's one worth making. Together we can accomplish the task.

Mary's Story

Mary, age thirty-three and married, is completing an MA in adult education while working as a staff trainer in a Fortune 500 company. Mary loves reading, skiing, working out, and cats; she's great at writing and making others laugh.

I remember so vividly when I started smoking. I have blurred memories about lots of my life, but my smoking history stands out very clearly. I was in sixth grade when a lot of my friends started smoking. At the beach, my best friend and I decided we weren't going to smoke. We thought it was really slutty, and we were not going to be sluts.

Next thing I remember is three years later and we're in my friend Terri's basement. I'm a freshman in high school. I'd actually made it through seventh and eighth grade with no desire to smoke and thought it looked stupid. I hated to see girls on the street smoking. So here we are sitting around Terri's piano; we have a pack of Old Golds, and we're learning to smoke. Her parents are out of town, and we're highly motivated to learn. I don't know what changed in those three years other than I began to identify myself more with grown-ups. Smoking took on more glamour. It was no longer street tough. By now all the girls I knew at school who were older smoked. It became for me a rite of passage. We all got very sick that first time on the pack of Old Golds, but we sort of knew that queasiness was part of the process and that we'd soon get over it.

I have some other early memories related to smoking. My friend Terri lived three houses away from me, and we used to walk back and forth between our houses. One school night in late fall, we were outside in the back alley, and four or five of us were smoking. We were still really new at it, and it was a very conscious act. After that, I was a smoker and wanted to be a smoker. All but one of my sisters smoked too, as did all of my friends at school. That first year I lost fifteen pounds. From then on, smoking was a very deliberate way of controlling my weight. I didn't sit around and think, gee, if I smoke, I won't get fat. But somehow I knew that I had replaced a lot of my eating behavior with cigarettes. I got an immediate payoff.

In high school, we smoked in the bathroom all the time. We passed those hot butts around. We could hardly hold on to them, they were so hot. Everybody knew we were smoking, but they didn't put much pressure on us to quit. They could have clamped down much harder, but they chose to ignore it.

I smoked all through high school and really got a lot of pleasure from being one of the crowd. When I got out of high school, I did a lot of drugs and alcohol, and smoking became a part of me. It became a part of my identity. I was a heavy smoker, and I felt more confident when I was with a cigarette than when I was not with a cigarette. I loved smoking for the fifteen years I smoked. I felt really powerful when I smoked, and the cigarette was sort of an extension of my mystique. I always had friends who smoked too. I didn't know people who were nonsmokers; I was not attracted to them. Smokers were a big part of my social network. Now that I think back, I did have one good friend who didn't smoke—Jimmy, who was crazy, wild, and wonderful. We ran around and did a lot of drugs and a lot of partying. He was a really funny, funny guy, and he never smoked. He always used to rag about people who smoked. He thought it was obnoxious, ugly, terrible, and unhealthy, but he was really in the minority. I can remember being amazed that he didn't smoke and surprised that he was so offended by it.

For years I smoked with intent, even though in the seventies, smoking was becoming unpopular. I made a conscious decision that I was not going to stop smoking because I had just stopped drinking. I got support from people who reinforced the notion that you shouldn't quit everything at once. I lived in a halfway house with thirty women, and twenty-nine of us smoked. The poor woman who didn't smoke was in a cloud of smoke all the time, and we just beat her up about it. "What do you mean you don't want us to smoke at the dinner table?" When I was in therapy, everybody smoked and it was great. It was something to focus on when everything was going awry. I smoked heavier after I quit drinking than at any other time in my life. I did more morning smoking.

I just loved cigarettes when I was in college and studying for exams because I would get up in the morning as early as three o'clock, make a pot of coffee, and sit down when it was perfectly quiet. I had a pack of cigarettes and my books, and I would study, smoke, and drink coffee until nine or ten o'clock. It was almost spiritual. I'd get a real chemical high from that early morning smoking. The early morning seemed to always be the time when the cigarettes and the coffee worked the best. I didn't like going to the library because I couldn't smoke there. I used to carry all these books around with me and go home where I could smoke and study.

About a year ago, I read some results of a study that concluded that nicotine had an effect on the brain that caused increased concentration. I knew it was true for me. The hardest thing for me when I was trying to make a decision to quit was that internal knowledge that smoking was a stimulant that was helpful to me. And I had said to myself, "I am going to smoke until I'm thirty." And that was when I was twenty-two. Whenever the subject came up, I said, "I'm not even going to consider quitting until I'm thirty." And then I smoked in total enjoyment and lack of guilt for eight years. I smoked my guts out. As I approached thirty, I got really nervous. But by then I started to have some consequences from smoking.

One night when I had stayed up writing something, I got so excited about what I was writing that I didn't want to go to bed. I stayed up and smoked and smoked. I slept maybe two hours that night. I was so excited about what I was working on that I got right up in the morning, put on a pot of coffee, and sat down to work with a cigarette, but I could hardly inhale, my chest hurt so badly. I noticed that often my chest ached, and I had to back off from smoking in the morning.

Gradually I started to open myself up to information about the harmful effects of smoking. I'd really cut myself off from that information. I didn't want to hear it. I had never thought about it. As I approached thirty and was having some consequences, I started considering a little more openly why smoking really was bad. I read a couple articles that blew my mind. I always worried about quitting because I always fretted about gaining weight. That entire eight-year period when I smoked so heavily, I used it very deliberately for weight control. I wasn't working out, and I wasn't taking care of myself in general. I was having a lot of conflict as I approached the goal to quit. I had a lot invested in smoking. I was just starting graduate school. And yet, I was also starting to realize how bad smoking was for me. Many heavy smokers I knew were quitting, and I was curious about that. I was hearing their quitting stories, and I was beginning to feel peer pressure. I didn't want to get left in the smoke. Smoking was becoming more unfashionable, and I was becoming more self-conscious about being a smoker.

The first time I quit smoking was after another night when I had been up late reading, writing, and smoking. I got up early in the morning with a bad cigarette hangover. I sat down, opened up the morning paper, and read an article about how the tobacco industry was beside itself that so many people were quitting smoking. They had come up with this new marketing strategy. They were going into third-world countries and selling cigarettes at a very reduced cost to get people hooked on them. Reading the article, I was appalled. I was just so disgusted knowing that by being a smoker, I was supporting that. Every time I lit up, I was encouraging or participating in the complete annihilation of human health. I quit smoking that day. I could not pick up a cigarette all day; I was just sickened by that article. I stayed off cigarettes for three months that first time. And that surprised me.

Right after I quit, my husband and I joined a health club. That was my reward. I was so out of shape that I was not able to swim two laps. I remember that first week after I quit; I was in an all-week workshop for graduate school. I was so out of touch because of withdrawal. I can remember listening to the instructor, having his words kind of come at me and go away, come at me and go away. That whole week I was so exhausted I'd go to bed right after I got home and sleep all night. I couldn't keep my eyes open.

What kept me from smoking was pride, just pride. I wasn't comfortable and I wasn't enjoying it. I was really preoccupied with smoking. I was proving to myself that I could do it. that was what kept me going those first three months. I cried all the time. I was really vulnerable those first six weeks and overly sensitive. I felt exposed when I was with people. But I knew it was due to withdrawal. My husband quit at the same time, and we would argue about any little thing. For about six weeks we were rageful. It calmed down toward the end of the summer, but then on a trip to Montreal, I started smoking. I was fed up with being preoccupied about not smoking. It hadn't gone away. It was there, and it was minute-to-minute. It felt like it was getting worse instead of getting better. I can remember going into a drugstore for cigarettes on the way to Montreal. Buying them was an escape out of this madness. I was uncomfortable. I was unhappy. I was rageful. I was not myself, and I was no longer glamorous. I felt odd and disoriented. I knew all I had to do was buy a pack of cigarettes and it would all go away. And it did. That was the scariest part. Within ten cigarettes, I was back into a complete, secure identity.

I felt so guilty. I never told my husband until after I had smoked a pack of cigarettes. I was really concerned about how I was going to tell him. So I figured I would quit again—either that or go to the bathroom a lot, because we were on our way to Montreal.

Four or five days into the trip, he started too. And then we had a wonderful time. We just smoked our way through Montreal. Things were just as hunky-dory as they'd always been. But then we tried to quit again on the way home. We were on this marathon drive back; we were going to do 1,600 miles in a straight shot. On the first day, we decided to quit. Eight hours later in a thrashing rainstorm in this little tiny car, we started raging at each other at two in the morning. By the time we got to Chicago, we were smoking again.

I smoked for another year and then quit again after my husband's dad got cancer. My husband quit immediately after he got the phone call about the cancer; he was through with smoking. I said right then and there, "I'm going to quit too, but I'm not going to do it right now." I felt like we shouldn't try to do it together. So three months later I finally quit. One morning I woke up with an incredible cigarette hangover and said, "That's it. I'm done." It was a lot easier because I also stayed off of sugar those first two months. The withdrawal was 100 percent less intense for me when I was not doing sugar. I was really surprised by how well I could manage the resurgences of the feeling of withdrawal. It would come, and I could trust it would go away. To know that it wasn't going to go on every day made managing it possible. I remember eating cake one night during that period. I got crazy with nicotine withdrawal after I ate the piece of cake. It was clear to me that the two were connected.

After about three months, I noticed that I hadn't thought about smoking lately. I felt liberated by that. I was much more ready to quit. I was focusing on the little bits of relief from the obsession with smoking that were actually starting to come, and I built on them. I remember the first time I was with someone who smoked and I didn't want one. I started noticing I was changing. I felt so liberated that I was becoming a nonsmoker and that I was released from the obsessive cravings. But this release didn't come until the third month. What was different this time was that I believed I would achieve it.

I got into aerobics. I had started working out when I'd quit before, and I'd maintained a lot of my commitment to exercise during that time. Working out provided me with significant physical relief. I had moments of serenity following a good aerobic workout, which gave me a great deal of strength and hope. When I quit this time, I realized that I really was powerless, but I trusted that if other people could do it, so could I. They served as my Higher Power.

I had about eight months of really good cigarette-free time, but then I started picking up cigarettes and smoking them. It only happened when I was with someone who was smoking. For six or eight months after that I'd have an occasional cigarette. At about this time, my sister, who smoked, moved in with us temporarily. I made a deliberate decision that I was never going to smoke with her. She only smoked on the porch, not in the house. Never did I bum cigarettes from her. I did bum from others on probably sixteen different occasions in a six-month period. But I didn't want to be a smoker. The motivation not to be one was enough to keep me from falling completely back into it after I'd been in those situations. But when I smoked one, I'd be having fun, and I would remember how much more fun it was for me to smoke. I would just pick up a cigarette and smoke it compulsively. And I would sidestep my decision to quit.

I smoked on Christmas day with my mother-in-law. She was sharing some of her feelings, and I was listening. I picked up one of her cigarettes and smoked it. I got so sick from the cigarette that I had to struggle to stay in the conversation. I had four puffs and put it out. That was the last time I smoked. I do have an incredible history with cigarettes. I have fantasies of smoking. I think my struggle will be lifelong.

It's hard for me to think that I could act compulsively and smoke again because I have so much shame. There'd be nowhere in my house where I could smoke without my husband having a fit. And I know so much about my health that I really don't think I could do it.

I believe that I'll start to enjoy the writing process without smoking, and that's what I'm going to have to focus on. I'll look for smaller rewards like writing a page or two, and then taking a break or eating an orange or something. I'll do some behavior modification.

For the last three years, I've never smoked a cigarette on my job, never. I sit and write and concentrate and plan and do all sorts of activities at work, and I don't have any problems not smoking. Even if somebody brought me a pack of cigarettes and said the surgeon general just changed his mind, I wouldn't pick one up at work. And I have found out that writing and not smoking has improved my concentration. I'm no longer getting wired. I may not start out as strong, but I have much more stamina to concentrate. I'm less edgy and less frustrated, and I'm more effective.

I've learned through all of my false starts that coming to terms with being a nonsmoker is really coming to terms with taking responsibility for my health and changing my identity. I had to stop and start again, but I was able to build on those experiences the next time. I needed to test the waters as I went along, and I gained confidence in the process. It was just a matter of sticking to my decision and learning about it as I went along and finding out what to expect. Nonsmoking is so day-to-day. It's sometimes a minute-to-minute kind of new identity. Not every person is going to be successful on the first attempt. I certainly learned that giving up sugar for six weeks reduced the severity of the nicotine withdrawal. I also learned that contact with other people, trusting other people's experiences, and listening to others' smoking stories helped me. When I was quitting, I felt it wasn't as intensive for others when they'd quit. It seemed others were always just sitting around drinking coffee and being casual about it. I had this sense that they were probably smokers who give up now and again and that they weren't ever really heavy smokers anyway.

The best thing about not smoking is that I did it. Nicotine doesn't have any power over me anymore. I think there were a lot of people who would have bet that I'd go back. I had that hardcore smoker image, and many friends thought I'd still be tapping a cigarette on an ashtray at age seventy. A real plus of not smoking is that I can go out and run for a mile if I have to. I can go to an aerobics class and not even be hurting. When I was struggling with quitting, there were days when one of my motivations for not having a cigarette was that I couldn't work out and smoke, and I loved working out. I loved doing it so much that it helped me not to smoke.

Another benefit of not smoking is that I love being somewhere and not having to worry about it. Every time I see a smoker stressing about where and how to smoke, I'm so glad that it's not me. No longer am I struggling to find an ashtray and an out-of-the-way place to smoke. It just gives me joy that I'm free. The hardest part for me has been gaining weight. I have gained fifteen pounds, the same fifteen pounds I lost when I started smoking.

It was very upsetting in the beginning, but I had to make a decision about my priorities. Once I made that decision, I was able to look at the weight gain as a part of my smoking problem. I look at compulsive behavior like this and I keep removing the roadblocks. I'm determined not to worry about it, although some days I feel frantic. I have compulsive eating habits that didn't make sense before. I didn't see them because cigarettes broke the compulsive eating pattern. I never saw myself as out of control over food, but I was, so I joined Overeaters Anonymous. I see it as really related to my smoking. And I'm finding relief and a spiritual direction. This time, I don't want to go back.

Jim's Story

Jim is a retired banker, age eighty-two, happily married and the father of four. His hobbies are auto travel, birdwatching, and lawn care. Jim is also an avid basketball and football fan who loves dancing to the big band sounds of the thirties and forties.

I graduated from high school when I was seventeen years old, and when I was eighteen, I left home and went to Logansport, Indiana, and got a job as a brakeman on a railroad. That was in 1922. My dad smoked as far back as I can remember, but I was in Logansport for two or three years before I started to smoke, and really only began because everybody else my age was smoking cigarettes. It wasn't too long before I started to inhale.

When I was out on the railroad, I smoked a cob pipe rather than cigarettes. I'll never forget one time when I was going between Moran and Sedalia. I was riding on top of a boxcar on a local freight train that delivered groceries, cartons, cans, and boxes of bread. The locals were only eight, ten, or twelve cars long, and they stopped often, so in the summertime, instead of getting in the engine or caboose to ride from one town to another, I crawled up on top of a boxcar and sat there smoking my cob pipe as we went from Moran to Sedalia. One time I noticed the smoke tasted awful hot. We always wore gloves, but I took the pipe out of my mouth and discovered that the whole side of the pipe was on fire. So I quit smoking a cob pipe. However, I didn't quit cigarettes. It was "manly" to smoke. Even though I wasn't a man yet, but a boy, when I smoked cigarettes, I felt like a man. And I continued to smoke throughout my life, for more than forty years with no problems.

Not until getting close to the time when I actually quit did smoking ever bother me. Although there was talk about lung cancer, I had no sign of any cancer in my lungs. I did have a touch of emphysema [COPD], so the doctor said, "Why don't you quit while you're even?" because the condition progressively gets worse.

Shortly thereafter, we were at Fort Wayne for my birthday, and we went out to this nightclub where there was a band that played mostly Glenn Miller music. We sat there and had a beer or a drink or something and I thought, boy, this is my birthday, this would be an awful good time to quit. I'll always remember it, although I don't remember the year.

Actually, I had quit once years before. I had kids going to college, and I got to thinking about how much it was costing me to smoke and how much better use I could put the money to even though cigarettes weren't high-priced then. So I quit. I didn't smoke for a year. I chewed a package of gum every day for weeks, instead of putting cigarettes in my mouth. But I crawled the wall sometimes, needing tobacco so bad I thought I couldn't live without it. But I did live, and when an urge came, I'd bite it off. I knew I didn't want to smoke again. But of course that didn't last forever. After about a year, I did start again, and I don't know why. I started and kept smoking steadily until the last time I quit, on my sixtieth birthday.

Like before, I had urges to smoke often. I was real nervous at first. I needed to keep busy, to keep doing something. On maybe a half-a-dozen occasions, I picked up my wife's cigarette and took a puff, never inhaled, just a puff. I'd get a mouthful and blow it out right away, and that was the extent of it. but I don't take puffs anymore, I haven't for years. Still, even now, when somebody smokes aromatic pipe tobacco, that sets me off something wonderful. I could just grab his pipe and start puffing, but I never have.

After quitting for a while, I soon noticed that everything tasted better than it did before. I think that's because the taste buds clear off. But I've never overeaten from nonsmoking, ever. And I didn't put on more than three or four extra pounds.

I've felt really good about not smoking. I'm proud of myself that I was able to quit at age sixty after having smoked nearly forty years, and that I was actually able to defy the urge to smoke. I just showed cigarettes a thing or two! I wasn't going to smoke, and I'm kind of proud of that.

I'm sure not smoking has contributed in a positive way to my long life. I'm eighty-two now, nearly eighty-three. When I think back on it, many in my family smoked. My Uncle George always smoked; Uncle Raymond always smoked. My granddad on my dad's side never did because he was a very, very religious fella. They told me he used to smoke when he was young, but from the time I knew him as a granddad, I never knew him to ever smoke. My dad smoked a pipe as I was growing up at home. It was during that time that cigarettes came out, and they were handier, quicker. So dad started to smoke Camels, and he smoked them until he died. Even my great-great-grandmother smoked. When I was three or four years old, Mom used to take us to see Great-Grandma Schaeffer, and she smoked a clay pipe. I used to think that was so funny, to see her sitting there in her chair holding her pipe, smoking. She always held it.

I miss cigarettes, even now after all these years. But I'm too bullheaded to give in and smoke now—and it's not just because of my emphysema. I've made up my mind it's a dirty habit. I quit and that's that! I just don't intend to smoke ever again. I do know this: If you're intimate with someone who smokes and you kiss them, you can smell it every time.

I feel great satisfaction at having been able to kick the habit, and I feel good about myself for staying away from cigarettes for twenty-two years. I only wish I'd live long enough to match the years I smoked with that many nonsmoking years, but I doubt I have that many years left.

A DOCTORS' DAUGHTER GETS SUCKED IN BY THE "COOL FACTOR"

Judy's Story

Judy, age thirty-five, is a published writer and editor as well as a former attorney, whose loves are a gardening newsletter she has launched, intimate times with friends, and home ownership.

My parents were both heavy smokers when I was growing up. I remember going on car trips and being sick to my stomach because they were smoking in the car. I remember begging them to open the windows. My early experiences said smoking was sickening.

Gradually medical reports were published about how bad smoking was. My parents, both doctors, were reading these reports, and they decided to quit. My mom quit first. My dad struggled with it, but they both had quit by the time I was in high school. The fact that they had quit probably prompted me to decide I was going to smoke. Besides, I thought it looked cool.

I remember seeing Lauren Bacall and Bette Davis in the movies and they smoked. They looked tough and cool, and I thought they were really neat. In general, it was cooler to smoke than not to smoke. I had a friend who never smoked simply because her mom was a real heavy chain-smoker. Her mom died while we were in high school. She had an operation for lung cancer and died right after the operation. But that experience didn't faze me. My grandfather died of emphysema [COPD], and I knew that was connected to his smoking, but that didn't faze me either. To me at fifteen, smoking was cool.

I remember my first cigarette made me dizzy. I tried to smoke without coughing so no one would know it was my first one. I was at our cabin. All of us kids snuck away to try cigarettes. I practiced a lot, checking myself out in the mirror to see how cool I looked. I practiced holding it different ways, as well as breathing smoke out through my nose and making smoke rings. It definitely was the thing to do with some groups of people, and it paralleled drinking. When I drank, I smoked. My sisters and I used to get away from the house and the parents to go drink and smoke. They would never have allowed us to do it at home.

When I was sixteen, I got my driver's license. My parents got us a car so that I could chauffeur my sisters around. That car became the place where we smoked. We used to call it the ashtray because it smelled so horrible. The smoke would come pouring out when you opened the door. My parents knew we were smoking, but they ignored it. I know they didn't want us to smoke, but they probably couldn't figure out how they would be able to enforce a rule against it. Every once in a while, my dad would threaten to take us down to the basement and show us slides of discolored lungs and lung cancer slides. But that didn't stop us. We only laughed at him. I knew that people died of cancer.

When I went away to college, I felt really emancipated, and I could buy my own cigarettes. Previously, even though I had a car, I was only sixteen, and you had to be eighteen to buy cigarettes. So we would go to certain service stations where they sold cigarettes from the service island because they wouldn't make you show an ID. We would buy Tareytons. After I went away to school, I switched to menthol cigarettes, Benson & Hedges 100s. I'd charge them at the school store on my student ID. I used to get a carton of cigarettes at a time, and I always protected my supply by having a carton on hand at all times so I would not run out of cigarettes. I rarely bought cigarettes out of a machine because they were not the kinds that I liked.

I figured I would smoke through college and then I would quit. I don't know where I picked up that idea. I don't know why I thought it would be cool to smoke in college and then stop. Maybe it had to do with my parents having quit. I knew my mom had smoked in college because we had some pictures of her smoking. I went to the same college that she had gone to so it may have been that I thought smoking was just something you do while you're in college. I didn't have much conception of what life was going to be like after college, but I did think, 'I'll smoke through college, and then I'll quit.' I didn't worry too much about how I was going to quit, but there's no question I was really addicted to smoking. I was smoking two to two and a half packs a day in college.

And the fewer my classes, the more I smoked. I wrote my thesis by writing and smoking and typing through the entire days, until one night I went to bed and I literally could not get my breath. I could taste ashes in my lungs. It felt like my lungs had turned to ashes. I knew that was real bad, but here I was in the middle of this thesis, and the cigarettes just seemed like a part of it. I needed them. Colds, sore throats, whatever, none of that convinced me to stop. Sometimes I'd cut back but I didn't stop.

Interestingly enough, most of my close friends were nonsmokers. I would not have tolerated the behavior from my friends that they tolerated from me. They didn't smoke, but I would keep an ashtray in each of their rooms, and I'd come in and smoke. I remember us going someplace on the train, and we had to sit in the smoking car. I was so insensitive. I wouldn't tolerate that now from people. I ask people not to smoke in my home and in my car.

Stop Smoking and Vaping Now!

But back then I wouldn't stop smoking even for a two-hour train ride. I remember smoking and drinking coffee, which I'd developed a liking for in college. My friends and I would sit around and drink coffee and smoke after meals and talk and talk and drink and smoke.

I loved smoking. It was doing for me what I wanted it to do, whatever that was, those early years in college. It didn't bother me that I was addicted, but I did expect to be able to quit at some point. I very much enjoyed my life. college was everything I dreamed it should be. I was smoking, drinking liquor and coffee, sitting around and talking with friends. And, of course, I felt invulnerable.

But I started thinking about quitting smoking in my senior year, right after my real bad experience while writing my thesis. I was having trouble catching my breath, and I knew that my lungs were in real bad shape. I had noticed that I couldn't run anywhere. I was having a hard time getting my breath after walking up a flight of stairs. Toward the end of my senior year, I decided to quit and so I got rid of my cigarettes. That lasted about a day. Then I decided I would have a cigarette now and then. My sisters were always occasional smokers; they smoked maybe three cigarettes a day. I thought I could probably do that. I went to some parties, and I decided that even though I was quitting smoking, I could have a couple. I remember borrowing a couple from somebody, and within two or three days after that, I was back up to two and a half packs a day. Having an occasional cigarette didn't work. It was a miserable failure. I didn't try to quit again for probably another year.

I'm glad in a sense that it happened that way, because I needed to understand that for some reason, I was either going to do two packs a day or I wasn't going to be able to have any. I certainly was not going to be able to just smoke at parties or just have a few a day. That wasn't the type of smoker I was. That's when I got my first clue that I was truly addicted. Before then, I enjoyed smoking and I never thought of myself as addicted. I thought I was real sophisticated and that people who didn't smoke were squares.

My friends and I would sit around and have philosophical discussions and talk about ending the war in Vietnam, and we'd go to demonstrations. We were very deeply and philosophically committed to things, but interestingly enough, not to our own bodies. We did not have respect for our own bodies and didn't know what we were doing to them by smoking or using LSD or other chemical substances. We were rebellious, so anything that society was doing, we were against. Besides, I didn't see myself going without cigarettes because I had always bitten my nails. I did that even when I smoked so I thought it would be terrible if I didn't smoke. What would I do with my hands? What would I do with my mouth? I always wanted to be doing something. I liked playing with cigarettes. I liked taking them out and messing with them and lighting them. I always had my lighter with me, and I did a lot of character playing that I enjoyed.

When I reached the point of really wanting to quit, something that helped me was yoga. I realized that it was difficult doing yoga and breathing exercises as long as I smoked. I couldn't take a breath down to the bottom of my lungs. Doing yoga cleansed me, and I felt like my breathing was getting better, but then I'd light up a cigarette, and I knew how contradictory that was. I finally got to the point when I said it's one or the other. I was either going to drop the yoga or the smoking. During college, I hadn't been into fitness activities of any kind. I had the required gym class, and I took as little of that as I could. I took bowling once to fulfill the requirements, but bowling didn't interfere with smoking.

My first attempt to quit smoking wasn't successful, and I continued to smoke for about a year after I graduated from school. I was more and more nervous about it because I was reading about how bad it was. There were many magazine articles, and I started to pay attention to them and was aware that something was happening in my lungs. I started to think a little bit about my grandpa and worry about that happening to me. One article in particular really scared me because it talked about menthol cigarettes and how bad they were for you. The menthol sterilizes the cilia in your throat, and the cilia, once they become paralyzed and die, are not replaced. The cilia's job is to act as a filter in your throat. The idea that I was killing something that wasn't going to be replaced really frightened me. I was doing something to my body that was not going to grow back.

I always had the thought that when I quit, I'd take control and be back to where I was before ever smoking. Now I knew different. When I thought of the thousands of menthol cigarettes that I had smoked, I really got scared. Every time I lit a cigarette, I was aware that I was doing something really harmful to myself physically. I was torn. I was getting to the point where I wanted to quit more than I wanted to continue. But I had to get to the end of that process.

There was a period where I didn't like the idea of smoking. I was talking about quitting, I was thinking about quitting, and yet I wasn't completely committed to it. Finally, I think the yoga was teaching me to feel better about my body. I believed it was good to take care of it and be respectful of it. I don't remember exactly when I decided to quit, but I got to the point where everything was right. I was ready to quit, and I threw away the many packs of cigarettes I had.

I was surprised that I wasn't more physically addicted. I thought I would have some real physical side effects because I'd heard about people being really crabby and having a hard time. And I didn't. It wasn't that bad. I didn't crave nicotine. I was surprised that it wasn't harder. I missed it a lot after mealtimes when I would normally sit around, have coffee, and light a cigarette. I felt a real pang that I couldn't do that anymore. But I continued the yoga, and I felt good about that. Pretty soon I started to notice positive things.

I had a little more breathing capacity when walking or running. I realized my clothes didn't smell anymore. I hadn't realized how bad people smelled who smoked. However, it was years

Stop Smoking and Vaping Now!

before I got around to having a nonsmoking house and a nonsmoking car and asking people not to smoke around me. One of the positive things that happened right away after quitting was the release from fear. I had really felt scared, especially about what menthol was doing to my system. I had been feeling uneasy every time I lit up, and I knew I was doing irreparable damage. The relief was there that at least the little cilia I had left were okay. Whatever are in there—only God knows how many are left—they're okay. I knew my lungs would turn pink again, and I would think about that. It felt good knowing my lungs were getting better and better.

Quitting smoking was lonely. I didn't have any support when I quit. I did it myself. Nobody was particularly interested. At the time, I didn't have a lot of ties with people. I was just ending a job, and I took a temporary job. I was planning to go to graduate school in England. My husband and I were breaking up, getting back together, breaking up, and getting back together again. I wasn't close to many people. In fact, I had no real close friends. It was a really unsettled time for me. I struggled, quitting all alone. I continued doing yoga, but I didn't begin any other exercise. I felt better about my body almost immediately. I gained a little weight, probably because I ate more sweets, but that didn't seem to be a big deal. My dad had used candy to help him quit too.

From the very start, I was committed to not smoking again. There were lots of times in the back of my mind when I wanted to restart, but I had this conviction that I would have to get all my powers together to quit again. Quitting had been hard enough the first time, so I didn't want to do that. This realization kept me from starting smoking again.

I haven't had a cigarette since. I can't remember for sure, but the last one was after I graduated. There was the temptation to smoke again when I went through law school. School and smoking went together. It seemed like I should be able to have a cigarette. But I knew if I lit up, I'd start smoking again. And, of course, the further on I get into my recovery from alcoholism, the more supportive people, including nonsmokers, around me who would challenge me about smoking again.

I know few people who smoke anymore. In fact, when I'm around smokers, I ask them not to smoke around me. It seems that everybody I've talked to has tried to quit; the reason they're still smoking is they haven't quite found a way to quit yet.

The benefits of not smoking are great. My health is so much better, and I know that whatever else happens to me, I'm not poisoning myself. Another thing that has become increasingly important is I've gotten rid of some of the other medicators too. Smoking wasn't the only medication.

Smoking is an incredible distraction. It keeps people away. I've asked people who smoke not to, not because the smoke was coming into my face, but because their hands were always in front of their face, in the midst of a cloud of smoke. Smoking makes connecting difficult. The lack of intimacy bothers me. I've started thinking about that and thinking about what I was trying to say to people when I was giving off clouds of smoke. I know now that I was clearly hiding and wanting distance from other people.

My sister is getting a divorce, and one of the reasons is because my brother-in-law is overweight and a compulsive smoker who refuses to quit, and she's afraid that he will die. She has decided she wants to be with someone who wants to live. And that's something that's important to me too. people who smoke are like people not wearing seat belts. It's passive suicide.

A tool that others might use to stop smoking is yoga. It was so cleansing. It was good to get a little bit in touch with my body. It's neat because it's not just mindless exercise, which is what really attracted me to it. I had to think about what I was doing. In yoga, you're a funnel of affirmations. You send affirmations, good messages, to different parts of your body, and the body responds. It's not just a passive thing.

Every once in a while, I wonder if I stopped in time. Am I going to get lung cancer? My grandfather had stopped smoking when the doctors told him he should, and he still got emphysema. It's not reversible. I'm glad I love myself enough to have stopped. I like being a nonsmoker. I don't think there's anybody left in the whole United States of America who doesn't know that if you smoke, you're killing parts of your body. It really is an out-and-out statement that "I don't care about myself." I'm glad I'm not saying that anymore.

Mike's Story

Mike, age thirty-nine, is a salesman by profession who is currently selling glass products. A married father of two, he loves racquetball and going to health clubs and is also an avid reader and political buff.

I smoked for the first time when I was nine years old. I was on the way home from the movie *Bambi* with my good friend Greg. I was an only child, and Greg had an older brother whom we idolized. He was about seven years older, and of course he smoked. Greg looked at me and said, "Mike, do you smoke?" I said, "No," and he said, "Want to try?" I said, "Sure." I was a straight-edge Catholic kid and all that stuff, but there was that part of me that needed to rebel, so we picked up butts off the street and we started smoking, although we didn't inhale until we were fifteen or sixteen. I smoked for five years, puffing without inhaling cigarettes. Greg would steal them from his dad, or we would pick the butts up off the street or else buy them from an older kid. We'd go and sit in the bushes and smoke.

I got into football and wrestling in high school, and as long as I was doing a sport, I wouldn't smoke. But then when I wasn't doing a sport, like when wrestling season ended, I started smoking again. Camel straights were what I smoked because they were macho. I thought, if I'm going to smoke, I'll smoke Camel straights. I won't smoke sissy stuff.

Funny, though, that I didn't miss them at all when I quit. I can remember how, every year on June 1, I would go down to Lake Calhoun and symbolically throw my cigarettes out the window, and I wouldn't think about smoking again until after wrestling was done for the year.

During this entire time, my parents never had an inkling that I smoked. My mother and my father were divorced when I was two, and Mom and I went to live with my aunt and uncle. My mother never smoked that I remember; my aunt didn't smoke either. My uncle smoked for a period of five years between ages fifty and fifty-five, and then he quit. My father has never had a cigarette in his life. My home life certainly didn't influence me to smoke.

I was always trying to walk the line between being this great athlete and being like everybody else. I never thought smoking was that great, but then there was a whole side of me that involved liquor, along with cigarettes. When I got to college, all hell broke loose. I began smoking, drinking, and partying all the time. By the time I entered the service, I was smoking about four packs a day.

I was a paratrooper, and I was running. I could run forever in the service, and I wasn't having any harmful consequences. In fact, when I got back home, I applied for a job and had to take a physical that included the Harvard Step Test. I had a resting heart rate of thirty-eight. I was in incredible shape, even doing four packs of cigarettes a day.

I got a job where I could smoke at my desk, so I had a place where I could smoke constantly. However, my next job was real estate, and one of the things they told me in training was not to smoke with my customers; and I thought that was a good idea because I knew some people were allergic to smoke and found it offensive. So I never smoked with customers.

My wife quit smoking in 1977. She quit cold turkey; we both tried to quit at the same time, but it was terrible for me. I just couldn't do it. It was so difficult, and the big thing I remember thinking was that when I'm not smoking, I'm not in control of my life. If I can smoke, that means I'm in control. That means I'm making the decisions. To not smoke is like Sister Mary Elizabeth telling me to do this or to do that. As backward as it sounds, to me, not smoking means that I'm not in control at all.

The first time I quit, a few years back, I switched to cigars for a while. Pretty soon I was inhaling them, so finally I said, if I'm inhaling these then I might as well go back to cigarettes, so I did. However, I still never smoked with customers. I always waited until I got home.

For years, I associated relaxing with having a cigarette. When I can sit in my favorite chair and light up a cigarette, then I know it's *my* time. The kids are in bed; the dishes are washed; the laundry is done. Since I quit smoking this time, I don't know what to do with myself. This is true even though I was down to only five or six cigarettes a day before I quit, except for on weekends, when I'd maybe go through a pack. I don't feel like I can relax, and I've been having trouble sleeping. My wife went through a sleepless period for quite a while too when she quit a few years earlier.

I also always associated bowel movements with smoking. I had a deathly fear that I would be constipated when I quit smoking. It didn't work out that way, but I really thought it might. I had gotten into a particular routine, and I suspected changing the routine would cause problems.

A lot of people wondered why I even wanted to quit since I smoked so little, but a friend I play racquetball with got me to thinking about it. We go back to when we were three years old, and he quit smoking ten years ago. One day we were talking about his upcoming thirty-ninth birthday. All of a sudden, we got into talking about aging, and the realization it gave me was like I was on a roller coaster and hit a brick wall. "I'm going to be forty years old." I started thinking about it, and I realized I wanted to be around to see my kids grow up. Besides, I figured that since I was down to only half-a-dozen cigarettes a day and only smoking in the evenings, I could easily quit.

I had another friend who was a three-pack-a-day Old Gold smoker. He and I go back thirty years. One day four years ago, he decided to quit. He had talked to somebody about acupuncture.

He tried it, and it worked for him. That was it. He has not had a cigarette since, and I figured, hey, I'm going to try that, and so I did.

The acupuncturist was from the Philippines. He was rather like a cherub in appearance. He gave me a physical and talked to me. He explained acupuncture and told me how he got into it. he said that he thought it was a bunch of bull at first, but he saw how even an internist couldn't do anything for many ailments and how medications often cause side effects. He was always trying to figure out what to do to alleviate some of the pharmaceutical side effects, so he began studying hypnosis. Over a period of years, he got more and more into it and found that with some people it helped. He said if you can find anything that helps in any little way when the medicine and the schooling fail, you latch onto it. Then a doctor friend of his went to a seminar on acupuncture and two years later was having success using acupuncture along with medical treatment. Finally he investigated it too and had good results with it.

So I took his treatment, and it's worked for me. I haven't smoked since. I've changed other habits as well. I started going to a health club, and I'm still playing racquetball. The only problem is that I'm still so orally fixated that I load myself with about two to four thousand calories between 8:30 and 10:30 at night. I'll eat a bag of Fritos, Cheetos, or peanuts. Because I'm working out, I've only gained about ten pounds, but if I can cut out the extra intake of calories, I'll lose the twenty pounds that I want to take off.

I still miss cigarettes, though. I love to read, and normally, after the kids had gone to bed, I'd sit down to smoke and read a book. I've been reading my present book for about two months! I just can't get through a book. I can't concentrate. I can watch television because that doesn't do anything to increase my urge, but I cannot sit down and read even the paper. I have a hard time because I association that activity with relaxation, and I don't have cigarettes to relax with now. However, I'm determined to stay a nonsmoker.

Nobody in my family has ever had cancer so fear of that didn't haunt me, but there's a history of being short, heavy, and prone to heart attacks. My Uncle Kelly and my Uncle Eddie both had heart attacks. When you have that history in your family and are prone to being overweight, you think about consequences. My grandfather is ninety-seven. Until about two years ago, he was working full days, five or six days a week. I don't know if I'll live that long, but I sure would like to see my kids get through college. And if not smoking will help, then I'm committed to it.

There are some real pluses to not smoking. It isn't all hard. One of the pluses is I can play good racquetball. All of a sudden I feel I can play forever again. There's a major increase in my stamina. I know there are other rewards, but I'm still trying to find them. right now, I still feel out of control because I'm not smoking. I'm sure it's just a matter of working on that and turning it around to feel I'm in control because I'm not smoking! I just haven't made that leap yet.

The big thing I've found out about quitting is that it's not easily done alone. It helps to take all the things that can be learned in support groups or in treatment programs and apply them to quitting smoking or vaping because nicotine is a chemical dependency just like any other chemical dependency. On the surface, behaviors with this substance don't seem to manifest themselves as negatively as with other chemicals. However, you're still doing things to your body that are terrible, and it's an addiction just as strong as any addiction. But I believe it can be licked, just like any other addiction, if you get help—whether from acupuncture or some support group. Quitting cold turkey means changing your whole attitude, and it'll never happen overnight. It's difficult. It's a difficult thing to do, but if you really want to do it, you can. There are benefits to quitting, but you sometimes need to talk to other people to remind yourself what those benefits are. The main one for me is I can now expect to see my kids grow up.

Ruth's Story

Ruth, age seventy-three, is the mother of seven daughters and one son, as well as grandmother of four girls and four boys. An avid reader and tennis player, she has a deep commitment to volunteerism through church and community organizations.

I think I was forced into smoking by circumstances. I really didn't like smoking when I first started in 1930. I started working at a bank when I was about eighteen, right out of high school, and I was working with a bunch of young women like myself. We had a restroom that was set aside for us, and everybody in that restroom was always smoking. It was the cool thing to do at that time. I tried unsuccessfully to smoke a few times and didn't like it. I would quit trying for a while, and then I would think, well, I don't really belong if I don't smoke. So I would go and get a pack of cigarettes. It took me a long time to learn how to smoke them.

Finally, by about 1932 or '33, I got pretty good at it. My sister Bea and I were really good friends in that period. We used to run around a lot together. We'd vacation together, and she smoked. I got pretty good at it with practice.

When I got married, I was sick a lot, so I just didn't smoke at all and quitting was easy. There was no stress about quitting. I don't think that I ever developed a really bad habit during that period at all.

By the time I started having babies, though, I'd smoke an occasional cigarette. I don't think I ever inhaled. I'd just puff on them in the evening, but I never smoked during the day when I was at home. I smoked sporadically. When we went out for the evening, everybody would be sitting around drinking, and then I would have a cigarette with my drink. It wasn't until the kids were pretty well grown-up that I started buying cigarettes for myself.

I think the kids leaving home led to more active smoking. I had less and less to do. And my husband was much busier in this period. He was in the real estate business, and he wasn't home a lot. He was drinking, and I was getting more and more isolated. I didn't have very many friends. I was alone a lot, and I filled the hours with reading. Smoking and reading just seemed to go together.

Cigarettes were my companion, my solace. But still I wasn't a heavy smoker. I never was a heavy smoker because I never really liked to smoke that much. I would get cigarette hangovers if I smoked more than two or three cigarettes in a row in the evening. If I smoked even half a package of cigarettes total, I'd have a terrible hangover from it. And cigarettes always sapped my energy. Instead of getting up and doing something, I'd think, well, I'll go have another cigarette. Maybe that'll make me feel better. I never knew smoking was dragging me down. During that time, I had an ulcer, and the doctor told me not to smoke. It is terribly hard on the ulcer. I'd go for long periods and wouldn't smoke because my ulcer was so bad.

In spite of how little it seemed, I was still smoking and had a serious nicotine habit. When we moved out of the city, I started smoking more heavily. I even started buying cigarettes and smoking on my own. Smoking became a real habit. It became part of my daily life. By this time, I even bought them by the carton. I smoked a pack a day, which was much more than at any previous time.

I tried to quit a couple times after my habit had become full-blown. I'd quit for maybe two weeks, and then I'd start again. I'd decide that smoking wasn't hurting me that much. Or sometimes I'd think the opposite. I'd decide that smoking was really harmful, and I'd just quit. I was seesawing back and forth all the time. Then one day I finally decided I wanted to really quit. I *really* wanted to quit. So I did. I didn't smoke for two years, and then, because of my husband's chemical dependency, I entered a family treatment program where unfortunately everyone smoked. My nicotine habit came back full force. I was spending more time thinking about cigarettes than I was about treatment, so I decided to start smoking again. I smoked from May until October, and then I quit again. I haven't smoked now for over two years.

The first time I quit smoking, I ate lots of sweets, which resulted in a gain of ten pounds. I quit cold turkey, and it didn't seem to be that big a deal. It didn't seem a very hard thing for me to do. It must have been, though, because when I started again during the treatment program, I had a psychological need to smoke.

The last time I quit, I hadn't really planned it. I just ran out of cigarettes, and I didn't buy any more. My husband no longer smokes, and it's easier not to smoke if nobody around you smokes. I did experience loss concentration. For three or four days, I couldn't settle down to anything. I would begin a project or begin reading or doing something with my hands, but I couldn't stay at it for long. I needed to get up and walk around and look out the window to get my mind off of what I was doing so that I could get a fresh start.

I missed my morning coffee, cigarettes, and the paper. That was a routine I had enjoyed. So when I quit smoking, I quit drinking coffee too. and I delayed breakfast. I would do something else right away when I woke up. Coffee, cigarettes, and the paper all went together. They were a habit, and when you change your habits, you change that compulsion.

This last time I quit, it was easier. I guess it was because I wanted to quit. I didn't have that leftover feeling that I ought to quit. I really *wanted* to quit. And that makes quite a difference.

Doug's Story

Doug, age thirty-seven, is a professional salesman who is currently selling glass products; married and the father of two, he loves racquetball and going to health clubs. Doug is an avid reader and political buff.

I started sneaking around to smoke in junior high. My dad was a smoker at that time, so frequently a pack of cigarettes would be lying around, and I would take a couple. I knew he wouldn't miss them. And then a friend and I would go off to smoke. Sometimes we went to the basement at my friend's house when nobody else was around. We also hid out under a bridge where no one could catch us. we tended to seek out-of-the-way places. We feared that if somebody saw us, they'd report it to our parents.

I continued smoking throughout junior high, but those of us who smoked by then were in a minority. Smoking was a real curious thing to do. I wasn't looked down on by my peers for trying cigarettes. It was a fun thing to try. We even tried smoking cigars. It was no big deal. However, when I got into high school, I started hanging around with a healthy group of kids, and I outgrew the smoking stage for a time. in fact, I didn't smoke again until college. I didn't have a desire to smoke during my early years in college, even though I hung around with both smokers and nonsmokers while living in the dorm.

And then, when I was in my junior or senior year, I began smoking again. My roommate was a pretty heavy smoker, and it seemed like I just stumbled into smoking again. It wasn't planned. Somebody offered me a cigarette in a bar, and I tried it. It was relaxing, and I enjoyed it, particularly when I drank. Smoking seemed to accompany the whole setting, the whole mood. I'd get a little buzz when I smoked, and I really enjoyed that part too, particularly the first couple of years.

In time I began to realize it was controlling me. It more or less took over my life. By my mid-twenties, I really couldn't live without a cigarette in the morning as well as throughout the day. at this time, I taught thirty miles from my home. my daily routine was to get up in the morning and have a cigarette first thing. Then I'd shave, shower, and eat a quick breakfast. During the thirty-mile drive, I'd enjoy a couple of cigarettes. And then at school, I'd have a cup of coffee and a cigarette before classes started. I'd smoke throughout the day at break time and at lunch. I was smoking a pack a day, except when drinking or socializing. Then I'd smoke more.

Before long, I was smoking out of need rather than enjoyment. The enjoyment kind of left. I could really feel the aftereffects in my lungs upon rising in the morning if I had smoked too much the night before. At the time, I was in pretty good physical shape, or so I thought, but I remember trying racquetball one time. I was so winded I could hardly catch my breath early on in the game. I was playing with a good friend who told me my smoking was my problem. I had played tennis pretty regularly all along, but tennis allows you to catch your wind after a hard volley. Smoking and tennis weren't that bad of a combination. Right up to the present day, I really don't care for racquetball because of that memory. I just couldn't catch my breath.

Because of the shortness of breath and sore throat and lungs, I did quit smoking once for several months. I prepared for quitting by using a special filter on my cigarettes which was designed to wean me away from the nicotine. I went through the weaning process for about four weeks. I got down to the last filter, and the accompanying directions said I should be able to stop—and I did. It was a relatively easy way to stop. I was off cigarettes for seven months. I put on some weight, and I didn't like that. I was out of shape, but this was in the late seventies, before the big push for everyone to get in shape had started. I was living in a town of about 10,000. There wasn't a YMCA or anything to join to work out. I even had to drive fifty miles to play tennis, so I didn't do that more than once a week, and I really didn't get into shape.

I didn't remain a nonsmoker for long. Stress drove me back to smoking; there was a lot of stress in my personal life. Smoking just seemed to be a good crutch to fall back on. I remember my ex-wife was disappointed that I was smoking again. I was putting in long hours at work, and I had a second part-time job besides. I needed something to get me through this tough period in my life, and cigarettes seemed like a good idea. That first cigarette, after not having smoked for several months, really shot right through my body. I got really light-headed and liked it.

For a while, I felt really good about smoking. It was a good companion. And then after only a month or two, I knew I was being controlled by it once again. I was no longer in charge of smoking. Soon I was back to smoking a pack a day, and I did so until about '82.

Somewhere in my mind, I knew I would quit again. My dad had quit when he was about forty or so. It was always in the back of my mind that I was going to quit too. having a role model like my dad, coupled with all that I had read and heard about smoking, convinced me that it was a foolish thing to keep smoking. In '82 I stopped cold turkey. I had just remarried that year. My wife didn't even know that I had stopped smoking until two weeks after I'd stopped. I was very low-key about it because of my fear that maybe I couldn't do it. I didn't really want to tell anybody in case I failed.

My process for stopping began with a decision to stop. I played with the idea a little bit. I knew there would be a day when I'd say, "This is it." That day came in May. It was toward the end of school. I was sitting in the teachers' lounge. I had stopped smoking for a couple days, and all of a sudden one of the teachers realized I wasn't smoking. He was an ex-smoker, and he gave me a little bit of reinforcement. I needed that.

I really craved cigarettes during the early period. I chewed a lot of gum. In fact, I *had* to have gum, and I chewed it for hours and hours. A couple months after quitting smoking, I started an exercise program; while I did get hooked on the exercise, I bounced around between activities a little bit at first. I started swimming, but the YMCA's hours didn't work well for me. So I tried running around the indoor track for a couple laps. I remember how it felt when I got to a mile, which was twenty-eight laps around the track. That was a goal I was proud of. I kept increasing the laps and added a little exercise on the weights. Finally I got to a mile and a half, and then two miles. I kept increasing it and got into a structured exercise routine. I'm still committed to my exercise routine, and I'm disappointed if I don't exercise at least three times a week. Usually I work out four or maybe even five times a week. My routine includes 150 sit-ups, 50 pushups, and a three-mile run. It's really important for me to hold onto that routine, and it keeps my weight down. When I left one bad habit behind, I picked up a really good one instead.

I do get urges every once in a while to smoke again. it's really unpredictable. Generally, it's when I'm around somebody who is smoking. I might be having a couple of beers with friends, and it seems like smoking would be fun. If it didn't so quickly control me, I would still enjoy smoking. I was laughing with a friend a couple days ago and saying that when I get to be seventy years old, maybe I'll start smoking again. Maybe that will be my goal. If I get to be seventy, I'll allow myself to smoke again. But when the urge surfaces now, I recognize it and let it pass. It stays with me for a minute or maybe ten minutes, or it might even last an evening, but I just wait until it passes. Most of my friends now are nonsmokers; but some of the kids I teach are really heavy smokers. They don't smoke in the school; they smoke outside of the building so I don't have to deal with their smoke.

There are many benefits to not smoking even though I still have an occasional urge. For one, I like knowing that smoking is no longer affecting my health. And I've begun to notice how smoke takes over a room. The smoke is everywhere, and quickly it gets into my clothes. I realize now I always smelled like smoke. I really enjoy not smoking because of our son. I feel good about being a healthy role model. And I like the exercise. I wouldn't have the energy to exercise as much if I were still smoking. Finally, I get a kick out of watching the cost of cigarettes going up, knowing that I'm no longer wasting my money on them. I see that they're now far more expensive than when I was a smoker. With the money I'm saving, I treat myself to little gifts that I wouldn't have bought before. That feels great. And I feel great!

Phil's Story

Phil, age thirty-seven, an attorney by education, is by choice a drug counselor in a major treatment center. Married and the father of a one-year-old daughter, he is an avid hiker, jogger, and fitness enthusiast who loves folk music as well as sports.

I didn't smoke much as a kid mainly because I always felt like I was supposed to be a good kid. I would occasionally sneak a few cigarettes from my dad's pack, but I always felt terribly guilty about it even though I knew he wouldn't know. He was a chain-smoker. When I was thirteen or fourteen, one of the neighbor kids used to steal whole packs of cigarettes from his dad, and we would go up in our tree house and smoke.

Even though I smoked once in a while, I really didn't care for smoking. One time I smoked four or five cigarettes in a row and got terribly green around the gills. I felt pretty awful, and that discouraged me from smoking much more for a time. In fact, in high school, I didn't smoke at all. I decided smoking was something punks did. But again, I was always trying to do the right thing and I was afraid of getting caught. Besides, my friends were all nonsmokers. I did not hang around with the wild guys at school.

When I really started smoking was my very first day at junior college. That day, our classes lasted about five minutes each. The teachers would introduce themselves and then give us some reading assignments and dismiss us. We'd all file into the student commons. That was my first experience in that kind of an unstructured situation. My high school had been very traditional. It was nerve-wracking that very first day meeting new people. It seemed everyone was smoking in the student commons, so I started smoking too that day and smoked the whole day long.

It felt pretty cool to smoke. I felt grown-up. Here I was in college, hanging around and smoking in the student commons. It felt great. It helped compensate for some of my feelings of inadequacy. It helped me forget how nervous and anxious I was, and I immediately began smoking a fairly substantial number of cigarettes, from a half to a little over a pack a day. That first summer, I decreased my smoking a little bit. I guess the habit wasn't deeply engrained; however, as soon as school started, I was right back into it. I think being away from the restrictions of home made it easier to smoke. My mother was a nonsmoker, and she didn't like it when I smoked. But I had quickly realized the joy of smoking because it helped me feel cool and not so anxious.

I smoked throughout college. I smoked until I was about thirty, and on the average, I smoked a pack and a quarter a day. On occasion, I smoked as much as two packs a day, but I felt that was too heavy, so I eased back. Actually, I probably always smoked between a pack and a half and two packs, but I like to think it was less. I still have some denial about how much I smoked.

The main problem for me with smoking was the money. I had very little money while going to school, and it was a substantial investment to keep myself in cigarettes every day. I wasn't aware or concerned about health consequences at that time, and I wasn't very athletic. I had a pretty sedentary lifestyle. I was overweight, I smoked, and I drank. And I enjoyed my life. For a long time, I liked being a smoker.

All the time I was drinking, I never had any serious thoughts of quitting smoking. I set some goals every once in a while—I said that since my grandpa had quit smoking at twenty-two, then I'd quit at twenty-two. But I never seriously tried to quit. Smoking was just too comforting to me.

The turning point in my life came after I got treatment for my alcoholism. When I went into treatment, I was in a state of paranoia, really frightened about quitting drinking. I was going to quit smoking, too, and all of a sudden I had all this fear that I'd really wrecked myself over the years. I was sure I had lung cancer, but the closest I came to quitting at that time was switching to a low tar and nicotine brand for about a day. I went back to my other brand, figuring if I'm going to smoke, at least it should be a good smoke until I quit. I didn't want to fool around with low tar and nicotine cigarettes that I couldn't taste.

With sobriety, my attitudes about smoking began to shift. I got to be less defensive toward people who confronted me indirectly about my smoking. When I was drinking, if someone made a comment about my smoking, I would inwardly get very angry and defensive about it. For instance, one time I ran my car into a ditch and this couple came along and picked me up. When I got into their car, I lit up a cigarette, and they asked me to put it out. All I could think was 'what a couple of jerks.' But the longer I stayed sober, the more I realized that there were some consequences. Smoking wasn't healthy. And it was expensive. I had hardly any money, and I was going to go into a training program to become a chemical dependency counselor. When I was still drinking, it had never dawned on me to try to be healthy or to try to live a healthy lifestyle. I had always lived a fairly unhealthy lifestyle. I assumed that was the way it would always be for me. But as my sobriety strengthened, I realized that I did have some choices about my lifestyle.

Cost and health weren't the only consequences for me. Another consequence was a spiritual one. I was consciously trying to work the A.A. Third Step. I tried to follow the will of my Higher Power throughout the day to have some kind of spiritual connection. But whenever I was smoking, I did not have that spiritual connection. When I was involved in a self-seeking, pleasure-oriented activity like smoking, I was effectively tuned out from the rest of the world.

I also realized the loss of freedom. I needed those cigarettes, and yet I wanted to be a healthier person, independent of compulsions. I liked going out in the wild to hike, but I realized that I couldn't. I needed to be near a drugstore. All of a sudden that felt really confining. At about the same time, I noticed that about two-thirds of the cigarettes I smoked did not even taste good anymore. They were smoked compulsively because I needed to have something to do. In actuality, they tasted awful.

I was also becoming more sensitive toward other people. I was upsetting some people by smoking. But I knew I couldn't quit smoking. I didn't have any idea how or why. It seemed overwhelming to simply quit smoking. But I also was aware that I could use the Twelve Step program to help me stop smoking if I became willing to stop. So I became more open and asked my Higher Power for the willingness to stop. I had never actually tried to use my Higher Power to help me stop smoking up until the day I actually stopped. I kind of knew inside that if I asked my Higher Power to help me stop, I would then have to make a commitment to really stop. Up until the day that I actually stopped, I had no idea I was going to quit. I only knew I was open to the possibility. I wasn't fighting it anymore. I was not trying to hang onto my smoking.

Then one day in July, I don't know the exact day, I woke up and had two cigarettes before I got out of bed; and the thought struck me that this was really stupid. Even though I'd done this countless times in the past, I realized I couldn't even get out of bed without having a cigarette or two. I was tired of the compulsion. I asked my Higher Power to help me stop smoking until eleven o'clock that morning, which was three or four hours away. That was as great a task as stopping for the rest of my life. I hadn't gone that long during waking hours without smoking for years. I stopped.

I made it until eleven and thought, well, I survived that, so let's try for the rest of the day. Again I asked my Higher Power to help me stop. I could definitely feel withdrawal. I was speaking rapidly. I was agitated. I felt almost giddy and high. I intentionally carried a pack of cigarettes around with me that whole day because I wanted to make it clear to myself that what I was doing was a choice. I've always hated to *have to* do something. Whenever I think I have to do something, I resist. I wanted to make it clear to myself that I had the choice to start anytime if I wanted to. But the pack of cigarettes stayed there all day, and it dawned on me that I actually wanted to stop. I went to an A.A. meeting that night and told one other person that I'd stopped, almost in a sneaky way, as if I was afraid to admit to the world that I was stopping. I was afraid that I would fall back.

I was glad that at the time, I was more or less self-employed, doing as much or as little work as I wanted to. I needed to concentrate on not smoking for two or three days. I was glad I didn't have any stressful situations to face. The first day was pretty bad. I was really agitated. The second and third day, I felt a sharp lessening of withdrawal symptoms. In fact, I was surprised that it was coming as easily as it was. I did not focus on smoking. Whenever the urge to smoke came over me, I used a little mental trick of pretending I was between cigarettes. That helped me get through the next two or three days. After about three days, I didn't feel any craving at all.

I needed an alternate activity in place of smoking, and I substituted exercise. At that point in time, I didn't know I was capable of really doing exercise. I focused on doing a lot of walking. I'd choose to walk rather than drive when it was a mile or two. Walking became a substitute for smoking. Now I have a compulsion with food, but I didn't substitute food at the point when I stopped smoking.

It is really good to feel free from the compulsion to smoke. I didn't appreciate how good it would feel until after the fact. I didn't know when I was smoking just how much I was missing by losing so much of my freedom to it. The further I get away from smoking, the more insane I think it is. I have not smoked for over six years, and I see nicotine as a very dangerous substance that kills people. I'm glad I'm not killing myself anymore.

In order to be successful at stopping smoking, I had to become open to an awareness of the consequences of smoking, both to myself and to others. Reeducation is needed. Most smokers plan to quit sometime. I always did. But I had to get really honest with myself and recognize that smoking is a pretty filthy habit. Smoke stinks up the world.

Secondly, I had to *stop* smoking before I could quit. All smokers plan to quit in a week or two weeks or three weeks or set a date, but more often than not, that doesn't work. I had to make a decision to stop today and not kid myself into thinking I could cut down. Cutting down doesn't work for an addicted person. Quitting sometime in the future doesn't work either. There has to be the willingness to stop *today*.

One thing that I knew instinctively after I stopped is that I can't smoke one cigarette. I don't even like picking them up because I still like the way they feel. I like the way they smell before they're lit up. Sometimes I like the first whiff off a cigarette when someone else is smoking. I know these are all pretty dangerous cues for me. There's certainly a part of me that's still a smoker because I'm such a compulsive person. I definitely consider myself a recovering smoker. I like a lot of things about smoking. It was a quick fix—a quick escape for me.

The best thing about not smoking is that I'm not actively killing myself. It's really special that I care enough about myself that I don't want to kill myself. I like living now, and I'd feel pretty bad if I was smoking and putting my wife into that much jeopardy. I realize I'm a role model, just as my dad was for me, and I like knowing that my daughter has a positive role model. All of my siblings have stopped smoking too. We don't have any smokers in the family right now.

Something recently happened that surprised me. Even though I haven't smoked for about six years, I started thinking about smoking again. I was watching other people smoke, and I thought I could probably just have a cigarette. I know that that's false, and I was able to look at the fact that there was some stress going on in my life, particularly related to my job, and I think I was starting to look for a quick fix again. Smoking used to take me away from the problem that I had at a given point in time. So what I had to do was admit that I was having those feelings. It's important to be able to verbalize that I'd been feeling like smoking. It isn't something that I really want to go through ever again. Smoking kills, and I want to live.

LEARNING TO HANDLE MY FEELINGS
WITHOUT SMOKING

Cindy's Story

Cindy, age thirty-seven, teaches junior high school English. Married and the mother
of two daughters, she was previously a dance instructor as well as a drug counselor.
She is a skillful tennis player who is committed to fitness and enjoys reading.

The first time I ever tasted a cigarette, I was nine or so. My mom smoked cigarettes, so I always associated smoking with women. I didn't know until I was much older that more men smoked than women. My dad smoked cigars and my mother smoked cigarettes. I thought cigars were male and cigarettes were female. My dad quit smoking when I was quite young. He just stopped, period. He never spoke about it ever again. Even today, if I were to ask him if it was hard to quit, he would say, "Well, that's just what you do."

The first time I smoked, my mom had tossed her cigarette butt in the bushes. Then she went back in the house. It was still burning, so I crawled into the bushes and smoked it, right in front of the picture window of the living room where my mom was sitting. She saw me puffing away. My sister, who is allergic to smoke now, tried it a couple times and coughed herself silly and hated it. She never did it again. But I remember liking it. When I was a little older, I went around picking up my mom's cigarette butts out of the ashtrays and smoking them way down. I couldn't figure out how my mom knew I was doing it.

I knew that my parents never wanted me to smoke, and I was the kind of daughter who did what my parents said. And so as I got older, I never smoked when all of my other friends were trying it in junior high school. I was very adamant against it. There was very strong peer pressure to do it, but I didn't. It was hard not to. I remember fighting it, and I never smoked in high school. I didn't drink either. I was one of those "good" girls. Even in my early years of college, I dated a boy who didn't smoke. It just wasn't a thing we ever did. I continued to resist really tough peer pressure. By the time I was a senior in college, I had broken up with that guy. I was searching for independence, and I think in my own mind, I was rebelling against my parents. I decided to smoke, and I liked it. I didn't buy cigarettes for a long time. I would just borrow one from a friend and smoke at lunch or something like that. It was just kind of fun. It never entered my mind that I would become hooked. Never. Nobody was talking about the health consequences of smoking back then.

I teach junior high kids, and they have this incredible belief in their own immortality. Even today, they have no concept of the dangers of smoking. They believe that they're in full control of their lives, and they believe that we're immortal—that we're untouchable. That was my belief, too.

Very quickly I moved to smoking a pack a day. I loved the taste of cigarettes. For eight years, I smoked a pack a day—consistently, from morning until night. The only time that I ever smoked more was when I went to parties. It's been ten years since I've smoked, but if they could invent a totally healthy, nonsmelly, nonmessy cigarette that tasted good, I'd smoke it because I like the taste so much.

I decided to give up smoking because I could feel definite physical symptoms. There was a tightness in my lungs and my throat. I could feel a bubble when I breathed hard. I got scared. It was there for a while before I paid a lot of attention. That was 1977, and more people were beginning to quit. Most of my friends either do not smoke now or never did. However, there was a time when almost everyone in my circle smoked. Several of them had already gone through stopping before I tried, and it didn't seem like it was a big deal to them. But to me it was—it was a very big deal.

The first thing I did was cut back from high tar cigarettes to low tar. I had smoked Marlboros and switched then to Kent Golden Lights. My husband and I were going to quit together; I would never recommend that for anybody, not ever. Because then you're not quitting for yourself, you're quitting for them. I remember going down into the laundry room and sneaking a cigarette. I didn't want him to catch me. Then I went to those filters you stick on the ends of cigarettes. That was helpful for me. It helped pull me away from the nicotine. By the time I finally did quit, I don't think the physical addiction was as strong. There was no question it was there, but I think trying to quit with my husband and realizing that wouldn't work made me see I had to stop cold turkey. I simply could never have another cigarette ever again. Even now, after ten years, if I were to have one, I know I'd start smoking again. I couldn't focus on quitting for just one day at a time. For me, it had to be forever.

Quitting was so horrible. I can still remember the pain. I started shaking. I couldn't concentrate on anything. I remember once I was sitting in my office at school talking to a student, and I had to get up and leave. I was nervous at work. I couldn't do my job because I was shaking so badly. I couldn't think about anything else. I remember telling a teacher who came into my office that I couldn't talk to her because I needed a cigarette so badly. I needed so much to talk to people who could understand what I was going through, but there wasn't a support system. I used to try to talk to my husband about quitting because I needed his support, but he wouldn't

Stop Smoking and Vaping Now!

talk to me about it. He said he couldn't talk about the subject. I still believe a better way to clear out and release some of those feelings is by talking to others. I really needed support because it was hard. It was really hard.

I felt very alone. People were happy for me that I was quitting, but I just didn't have the sense that I could talk about my feelings to them. It made me very sad to reveal my feelings. I felt so isolated at the time. I was feeling so out of control of my life.

My physical reaction lasted for eight or nine days, and then I started not to shake as much and I could concentrate better. But that first eight or nine days were so hard that I will never start smoking, because I never want to go through that again. it was the most painful thing I've ever done. I hesitate to share that with others because I don't want to scare them off. It does get better, though.

About two or three months after I quit, I awakened in the middle of the night and couldn't get back to sleep. All my life I'd been a wonderful sleeper. Sleep has been very important to me. I like ten hours of sleep and sleeping late on the weekends. But I began having insomnia. It lasted for a year and a half, and it was horrible. I would have no trouble getting to sleep, but would awaken in the middle of the night and be up for anywhere from one hour to four hours a night. At the time, I didn't associate the insomnia with not smoking.

After about a year of this, my husband and I started going to a therapist. Since I couldn't sleep, I was going berserk. Seeing a therapist opened up all sorts of issues that weren't necessarily connected to the insomnia. We discovered my insomnia wasn't really the problem. The problem was depression and low self-esteem. My sleeping problem was a barometer of how I was feeling about myself. It wasn't *the* problem; it was only a symptom.

What I came to understand was that my insomnia surfaced when I was desperately trying to get control of my life, and of my self. It felt like I was trying to hold on. What I traced back to smoking was the realization that I blew out negative feelings through exhaling. I had never been taught how to deal with negative feelings while growing up. Negative feelings weren't something you brought up or dealt with in my family. And so long as I smoked, I could get rid of them. But as soon as I quit smoking, I had no release for those feelings. And so they stayed inside. After two months, they had to come out. What the therapy was for me was learning how to get in touch with the feelings. I remember saying to people, "I don't get angry." But I did. However, anger was considered wrong in my family. In my family's belief system, only an out-of-control person gets angry, and the greatest thing you can be is in control. It was almost a moral judgment. People who were out of control were less moral than those who were in control. Being in control was extremely important to me. Therapy dealt a lot with these issues of control for me. Smoking had allowed me to push all of that away. I never had to come to grips with any issues because I smoked and got rid of my feelings, or so I thought. But they were obviously there, building up. For me, it was horrible to quit smoking, not only because of the physical reaction, but due to the pain of therapy too. But in the long run, the therapy was the most wonderful thing that ever happened to me.

Other than the changes wrought by therapy, I didn't see any rewards from not smoking for about six months. I'm a tennis player and a dancer; I taught dance for a long time. My endurance came back, along with my lung capacity and my stamina. I didn't get winded the same way. And that gurgle in my throat started to go away. That gurgle was the most frightening thing. If I took a deep breath, there was a catch in my throat. That left after about six months. I knew I smelled better because I could smell people who were smoking, and I realized that's what I had smelled like.

Probably because I'm a teacher, I think a lot about how people are educated. And based on my own experience of quitting, I don't believe the intellectual approach is the way to teach others to quit. People have to have information, but you're never going to stop kids from smoking or keep any person from smoking by just giving them information. I always knew gunk came out of cigarettes. I knew very well that all that was inside my lungs, but that didn't keep me from smoking.

I stuck by my emotional decision because I kept remembering the pain that I'd experienced, and I couldn't allow myself to go through that pain again. I still cannot concentrate for as long as I used to. It's harder for me to read a book now, and it's been practically ten years. Since I quit, a book has to be much better to hold my interest. I used to use cigarettes for rewards. I'd be correcting English papers, and after maybe five papers, I'd have a cigarette. Now, the reward might just be getting up and taking a little break. I try to find some other little thing that rewards me.

The best part of not smoking is the freedom. When I was going to therapy, one of the things I found out was I didn't have a lot of control over anything in my life. A friend of mine back then gave me a button that said, "Thanks for not smoking." She said she wanted to remind me of the areas where I do have control. I remember crying when she gave me that because it was wonderful support. And I also did learn that there are other areas where I don't need control and that's okay. Smoking felt like this monster holding me, and it felt amazing to be free of it. I no longer feel trapped now.

For a long time, I had dreams about smoking, lots of dreams. In the recurrent dream, somehow or other I had forgotten that I had quit smoking and had moved back to square one again. It was a feeling of real fear. I was disappointed in myself because in the dream, it wasn't a conscious choice. It was something that just happened and so it wasn't my fault; the feeling I got from the dream was all of that for nothing! And then I'd wake up and feel tremendously weak.

I think the hardest time was when I wasn't seeing any reward at all. It's kind of like having a new baby. The first few months after the baby is born are often horrible. There are few rewards, only dirty diapers and crying. Then all of a sudden at six weeks old they smile, and it's just in time. You can be right at the very end of your rope, and then they smile at you. One little tiny reward is enough to help you get going, and then you get more and more and more, and you realize that it's only going to be getting better, not getting worse. It's the same with not smoking. Those little rewards were enough to sustain me.

Talking to former smokers and asking them to listen is wonderful support during the hard times. It would have felt less lonely for me if I'd been able to do that. I think a big thing for me was to try to figure out why I smoked. My husband and I smoked for very different reasons. Therefore, our quitting needed to be very different. I smoked for tension release. I didn't smoke for pleasure. Although I liked it, I sure didn't smoke for pleasure. There were about two cigarettes out of the day that were really pleasurable. Sitting down with a cup of coffee in the morning and smoking that first cigarette: that was a pleasure. And sitting down with a drink and a cigarette later in my day was really pleasurable.

The smoking part of my life seems so long ago. I don't ever think about smoking now, and I never thought I'd get to this point. for a long time, I'd think about smoking, but then the feeling would pass. To ever start again would mean quitting again. and it was too painful. I'm willing to go through pain if there's a benefit, like with childbirth. I'm willing to do that, but with smoking, there's no benefit.

Virginia's Story

Virginia, age thirty, is a medical office staffer by day an avid reader during her free time. Married and the mother of a newborn son, she is a warm and compassionate woman who is a talented seamstress.

I started smoking really young. I probably smoked my first cigarette when I was ten or eleven. It wasn't really clear-cut, my going from being a nonsmoker to a smoker, because there was so much smoking going on at our house. Both my mom and dad smoked, and I had six older sisters. It was cool to smoke. I can remember that by the time I was in eighth grade, I was a regular smoker. I don't remember how much I smoked, but I was buying cigarettes, even though I only smoked with my friends at first. I started smoking with my sisters when we were supposed to be in church on Sunday morning. I smoked with my sisters, but I didn't do very much with them socially because I was too young.

My friends and I mostly smoked outside, and whenever somebody's mom wasn't home, we'd have smoking parties. I remember the house we lived in had a loft in the garage. My dad didn't park his car in the garage. Nobody ever went in there, and it was used for storage; it became my clubhouse. It was great—wonderful for smoking.

At school, my friends and I smoked in the bathroom. I can remember getting suspended for it in the ninth grade. My mom and dad were in Mexico. I was really stupid because I didn't know the school's rules. If you were suspended, you had to bring a note from your parents and were required to pay a ten dollar fine. I forged a note from my mother, but I didn't pay the ten dollars. Before they would let me out of school at the end of the year, they said I had to pay the ten dollar fine. So my mom found out, but she didn't openly acknowledge my smoking.

I started smoking pot around that same age. Two of my sisters, Mary and Rose, were still at home. When Mom would find pot, she would take it and flush it down the toilet, never saying a word about it. It was pretty weird. I don't think my mom ever acknowledged that I smoked, and I don't think I ever smoked in front of her until I'd graduated from high school and moved out, after which I was an 'adult.'

I can remember feeling so powerful when I first started. It was a way to be cool, to be doing what other girls that I admired were doing. I don't think I ever thought about quitting or thought that smoking wasn't good for me until I was seventeen or eighteen, and then I fell in love with a fellow who didn't smoke regular cigarettes, but smoked pot constantly. It was 1973, and I was a hippie; I did not shave my legs, and I was part of the "go back to the land" movement. Since that was my whole ideology, I did quit smoking with hardly any struggle for about a year.

We hitchhiked across the country the year after my friend and I graduated from high school. He dealt dope mostly for a living, and I worked. In those days, you could live for a lot less on the road. We left town with about six hundred dollars, and that lasted for three months. And we lived well by our standards. We never paid to sleep in a hotel. Sometimes we'd give people money so they could buy gas if they needed it; most of the time not. Gas was still only thirty cents a gallon. We bought pot all the time, and we bought concert tickets. We were nomads on the move, following the good music, and it was fun. One day, though, we had this big fight, and I went out and bought a pack of cigarettes.

I really had to work at smoking again. The first cigarettes did not taste good, and they made me feel nauseated, but I smoked for five more years.

Smoking has always been an emotionally reactive thing for me. It's almost like a haven, a safe harbor to go to. I feel such a sense of emotional loss whenever I quit. I always feel as if I've lost the best friend I've ever had. It isn't like that twenty-four hours a day, but I get rushes of this really emotional feeling of loss.

During those next five years, I wanted to quit smoking many times and actually did quit drinking and using other drugs. Mark and I broke up, and my life changed a lot. I had a million incidents of quitting for two weeks, quitting for three months, quitting for twenty minutes. But I didn't have any plan to help me quit. I had quit once successfully and with very little trauma, so I didn't figure I needed a strong support system or a backup plan. I wanted to be able to just do it. I didn't want to chew Nicorette gum or go to Smokers Anonymous or be hypnotized or get acupuncture treatments. I said, "Well, I can just do it."

However, I was so emotionally dependent on cigarettes that I just couldn't cope without them. And for every time I quit, there was a different scenario of why I started again. After I had moved to California, I quit for about six months and then started smoking again the week before I got married. I had loved not smoking. It felt really good, except that I gained about thirty pounds, which I found really traumatizing. I had quit in May. We were planning the wedding. I had to pick out a dress and plan the wedding, and I felt like this big, huge, fat pig. I dieted all summer and exercised vigorously, yet still I did not lose any weight. I was completely, utterly despondent, so I started smoking again, and then I felt terrible, especially because my fiancé had quit about two years before.

When I had quit earlier that spring, we were living together, and he had expressed over and over how much he loved living in a house where nobody smoked. I knew he was bummed out that I was smoking. I smelled like smoke, and I tasted like smoke. I felt really guilty, and I hid my smoking from him for a couple days; then I said, 'the heck with it!' I told him I was smoking, and we made some agreements about smoking in the house. I didn't smoke in the bedroom. I continued to smoke until October. That month, I learned that I was pregnant, and I had always said that when I got pregnant, I would quit smoking. Well, it wasn't that easy. Even after finding out I was pregnant, I continued to smoke for a couple of weeks. Then I declared, "Okay, this is it!" But I was only able to stop for three weeks. I would buy a pack of cigarettes, feel guilty, and stand over the toilet and rip them all up, then flush the toilet. And then the next day I'd do something similar. I was out of control. It felt like I was truly powerless. It took me beating myself over the head with that for two months before I finally got it that I was totally powerless. Then I realized I could use the Twelve Steps to help me.

The first three Steps of the Alcoholics Anonymous program really helped. I got it that I was powerless. My life was unmanageable around cigarettes, and I was acting insane. I knew from previous experience that if I called upon my Higher Power, it would really come through and give me the strength I needed.

One night, I went to my A.A. meeting and talked about it. I told the truth and got lots of support. When I realized that I could not quit smoking, that I was so addicted it was out of my control and I could not quit, then I was able to stop. That was about three weeks ago, and I haven't smoked since.

Unfortunately, I still think about smoking a lot. I quit because I got pregnant, and most of why I don't smoke right now is because my baby is growing inside me. Lots of times when I want a cigarette, I'll say to myself, "I can smoke in six months, after I've finished nursing." Some days I think that I'm going to want to smoke some more, and some days I know I'm totally done.

It's become so socially unacceptable now. And my father, who can hardly breathe due to emphysema [COPD], is a real dash of cold water. I want to totally deny that there are health consequences. I've seen data that smoking can cause the placenta to break away from the wall of the uterus. Learning that my smoking was life-threatening to my unborn baby really got to me. Research indicates that mothers who smoke have smaller babies and that there may be long-term health consequences for those children. They may never be as strong physically as children of mothers who don't smoke.

Stop Smoking and Vaping Now!

These last few weeks, the urges to smoke have come, but they haven't been overpowering. And what is once more so clear to me now is how powerless I am. I can't just take a drag off somebody's cigarette because my life immediately goes out of control. It's scary to think that I might have to continue to go through this.

One problem is I don't ask for help when I want a cigarette. If I wanted to drink, I would ask for help. Tobacco is worse for me. It feels like I get crazier around cigarettes than I do around alcohol. I guess part of it is that there are still places where I can go and smoke. There aren't any places I can go anymore and drink or do other drugs without somebody telling me to stop. But you can still smoke. There are enough people around who will tell you it's okay to smoke.

It feels great today to be a nonsmoker. I love it that I can breathe, that I can have a clear conscience right now. Having my conscience clear really affects my relationship with my husband. When I smoked openly, like before I was pregnant, I noticed that if he and I were cuddled up on the couch being cute and I wanted to smoke, I would move away and smoke pit the window of something. I didn't want to smoke him out. Smoking was really distancing. Then right after I smoked, I would stay away because I knew I really smelled like smoke. Smoking has very much been a barrier between us.

One helpful thing I've been doing lately is a lot of deep breathing. When I'm conscious of my breath, I notice how good it feels to have clear passages and clean lungs. I know how sweet this air is when I'm not smoking. I have also used a subliminal tape. One side is a visualization meditation with relaxation along with some information about cleaning out your lungs and feeling good about not smoking and some positive reinforcement. On the other side, you hear the ocean, and subliminally you are reinforced not to smoke.

I'm not sure if my struggle is really over. I think it will come up strong again after this baby's out of my body. I feel like I'm a committed nonsmoker and loving that part of the time, but not always. I really do see it as a process. I watched my sister when she quit. It took her two years to really be done. To look at it as a process is more hopeful for me than to see it as something that defeats me.

For the majority of people, it's not just black and white; for most, it's a series of times when one is stopping and starting. And hopefully stopping again.

Bill's Story

Bill, age fifty-seven, is a divorced father of three sons who is now the proud grandfather of a little girl. A computer expert by profession as well as in his off time, he loves a rigorous game of racquetball.

I started smoking when I was twelve or thirteen because I saw other people, including my father, doing it. I stole them, to begin with, from my dad. At first, I snuck around to smoke, but by the time I was fifteen, I was a regular at it. I had a job in a grocery, so I got all the cigarettes I wanted. Very quickly I got to be the "big man on campus" because I could provide all the other guys with cigarettes. We all smoked, but interestingly, many of my friends never really got hooked on them like I did. I think it's just another example of the addictive personality. it felt good, so that's how I got started. I didn't make a decision to be a smoker, but it quickly became a habit. When I was in the service, everybody smoked. I don't think I knew anybody who didn't smoke for years. Only the last ten or fifteen years, probably because of all the cancer scares, have friends of mine quit. In past years, everybody smoked.

The big joy of smoking for me was sucking in a lung-full of smoke, particularly the first one of the day. It gave me a little high, but after two or three cigarettes, it was more of just a habit for the rest of the day. I think very early on I decided smoking was a terrible thing to be doing and a nuisance, not to mention expensive. I was a two-pack-a-day guy from age fifteen on. It had become a habit, and if one cigarette felt good, then two felt better. Also, I was a nervous person, and smoking became a nervous habit for me. When I wanted to concentrate on something, I'd have two or three cigarettes.

Not until my later years of smoking, when it became a noticeable health problem, did I seriously begin to question what I was doing. By that time, in many places where I planned to smoke, I couldn't smoke. More and more often, people were objecting to it. For a time I smoked pipes instead of cigarettes. I thought pipes were healthier. Unfortunately, I was doing a lot of air travel, and of course, on planes, I couldn't smoke a pipe, only cigarettes. But I never consciously thought of quitting until I was convinced that smoking was a hazard to my health, and that was after I'd started with Alcoholics Anonymous. Like a lot of people in A.A., I decided to quit everything all at the same time. I went into a halfway house after treatment for alcoholism with plans to quit cigarettes and coffee. The first thing they told me was that cigarettes were available, and I didn't have to pay for them. I quickly got over my plan to quit smoking.

People who started smoking back when I started never questioned whether it was good or bad for you. In fact, I'd discovered some real benefits. Smoking calmed me down. It gave me something to do. And it was preferable to drinking. Until I became convinced it was a health hazard, it felt like a positive factor in my life, even though the financial cost of it grew and it did get people mad at me, in particular my ex-wife because I got burns in my clothes. She always complained about the smoke too. I never believed her until I quit. Now, when I go into a place where people smoke, I can smell it. I sure didn't believe that when I was smoking, though. I was surprised to realize how much I had stunk as a smoker.

In actuality, it took me a long time to quit smoking. My first plan to quit was in 1969 when I went into the halfway house after rehab. I didn't quit, though. But after I moved to Texas in '70, I had to start seeing doctors the next year because I couldn't breathe. They never told me I had emphysema [COPD], but they put me on medication to help me breathe easier. I switched to pipes for a while, and then I rolled my own for a time because the process is tedious, and it takes longer to get a cigarette. I knew I'd smoke less doing it that way.

The doctors told me to quit, and I knew I had to. I believe that was back in '71, but I was so addicted it took me much longer to do it than I'd figured on.

Back in Minnesota, a year or so later, I went to a nonsmoking clinic with a friend. We were trying to quit altogether, but neither of us was successful, although at first I believed I would be. The smoking clinic employed a behavior modification approach. It was partly similar to A.A.; we went to meetings once or twice a week and talked about our experiences. We were to taper off from smoking by having to smoke one less cigarette every day. it seemed to work for a little while, but I never went even twenty-four hours without a cigarette except when I had bronchitis. It didn't last. In a matter of weeks, I was back up to four or five packs a day.

For a time, I was on and off, always trying one thing or another to quit. I tried graduated filters, the kind where by the end you can hardly pull air through it, let alone draw smoke. I switched from regular cigarettes to filters with low tar. In the later part of the process, I was smoking Carltons. They were still more than enough to stir up my emphysema [COPD]. Actually, I was never diagnosed as having that condition in the late '70s; I was simply on medication for breathing. I had to take a pill twice a day, and if I didn't take them, I might as well have stayed in bed because I couldn't breathe or move around. There was a rather long period when I knew I had to quit.

Although I had in general liked smoking, I did have some dangerous consequences, but they also resulted from my drinking. Once I passed out from being drunk while I was smoking. I had only been married a short time. I burned the mattress up and burned a hole in a fancy mattress cover. My ex-wife carried that cover around for fifteen years and used it to guilt me about my smoking or whatever she wanted to guilt me about. Aside from that, I got real good at smoking; for instance, I could light a smoke while riding a motorcycle going sixty miles per hour. I never figured out how to smoke them underwater though.

By the time I decided to quit, I'd started looking into hypnosis. I knew about acupuncture and aversion therapy. And I decided to pick the cheapest method for quitting first. I was aware that maybe I couldn't get rid of the addiction, but I was sure going to try everything that was available to do it. Hypnosis was what I tried, and fortunately, it worked.

The hypnotist was a medical doctor from the university. I did a little bit of research on it before I made my appointment. I had to wait a couple of weeks to get in, and I was determined to give myself any possible edge to improve the odds. The day before I was to be hypnotized, I went through my apartment and collected everything that had anything to do with smoking: my matches, my pipes (I must have had seventy or eighty pipes), half-a-dozen pipe racks, lighters, pipe dampers and pipe cleaners, tobacco, and a cigarette rolling machine. I collected a whole box full. I put everything I could find in there except one pack of cigarettes I needed to get me through to my appointment. I gave it all to the Salvation Army—everything. My goal was that when I got back home from the hypnosis session, there would be nothing that I could smoke, literally nothing. I smoked my last cigarette walking over to the doctor's office. I threw the rest of the pack in a garbage can.

The hypnosis session was very interesting. The doctor gave a nice long explanation of what he was going to do and why, and of how he felt it was going to work. He told me that the main problem for people smoking isn't the physiological addiction, but the wired-in habit. He pointed out that you make this arm motion of lifting a cigarette from an ashtray to your mouth maybe five or ten times per cigarette. If you're smoking a hundred cigarettes a day, you're making that motion four or five hundred times. He said that I had to do something about that motion. The point of his hypnosis was to remove the need for making that arm motion. He said, "I can't do anything about your nicotine addiction. You're going to have to live through that. But I can take care of the arm motion and give you a suggestion that you don't need to make that motion again." What he said made a whole lot of sense to me. He asked me as an afterthought if I was at all worried about my weight. I responded that I'd been trying to lose weight for a long time. He asked me how much weight I wanted to lose. I said ten pounds would be nice. "All right," he answered, "we'll do that.

I swear I was completely aware of everything that was going on the whole time I was under his "spell." But I'm told one always thinks that. Anyhow, the bottom line is that I have never once smoked since. And in the first month from when I quit smoking, I lost ten pounds! I did gain it back, but that was three or four years later. My friend was quitting at the same time, and she's still mad at me because she gained the ten pounds that I lost. Hypnosis worked for me. I've sent several people to that doctor, and it's been about 50/50; it works for half the people that get hypnotized, and for the other half, it doesn't.

My craving was gone completely. I thought about cigarettes occasionally, but I didn't have to smoke. It was similar to what happened for me with my drinking. I tried for years to quit. I went to A.A. for a year while drinking. Then I was able to quit when the right time came. I don't think either addiction would be gone if I hadn't tried all those ways to quit, but when it finally happened for me, it was clear-cut. There were no physical symptoms, no withdrawal.

In the years since I quit smoking, there have been some definite physical changes for the better. One that I never expected was I used to have headaches practically every day. I don't have them anymore. I asked my doctor about it, and he said it's not uncommon for people to quit having headaches after discontinuing tobacco. And of course, I can breathe. I don't have to take that medication anymore. I'm calmer, I think, than I used to be. I've had to learn to deal with the nervousness without having to use a chemical. I've begun to rely on spiritual meditation rather than medication.

The financial benefits of not smoking are great. I was smoking as much as five packs some days, so the savings really added up before long! I can remember being so delighted on that first day and second day of not smoking. I could see how it was possible I wasn't going to have to fight those negative consequences anymore. Quitting offered a pure benefit once I got there.

I'm a very grateful, nonbelligerent ex-smoker, and I'm very compassionate toward people who have to smoke. It hurt me so much for so long and it was so hard for me to quit that I can't help but feel sorry for anybody who's going through it.

It's so much more comfortable being a nonsmoker. There are so many places where smoking is discouraged if not flatly prohibited. It's kind of nice not to have to worry about that kind of thing. I don't have to worry about whether I'm in a smoking or nonsmoking section. It's a freer, more comfortable way to live. I no longer have to check my pockets when I go out to see if I've got enough cigarettes or get up at three o'clock in the morning to go to the store. The world's becoming more and more a nonsmoking environment. So many workplaces now completely ban on-site smoking. It's easier—it's really easier in the society that we live in today to be a nonsmoker.

"BEFORE I QUIT, I ONCE MANAGED
TO LIGHT MY HAIR ON FIRE"

Kaye's Story

Kaye, a forty-seven-year-old bookkeeper, is a whiz at bridge and quilting. Kaye is the kind of person who always takes time for friends in need of emotional support.

I grew up with smokers. Both my parents smoked, so it seemed like an acceptable thing for people to do, but I disliked it intensely when they smoked in the car. Sometimes I would get violently ill from it. Because of that, I made a decision when I was still a child that I would not smoke. However, that decision fell by the wayside when I went away to college. Their no-smoking rule invited my defiance. It was grounds for dismissal if we were caught smoking. I waited until the last week of school my first year before smoking, but then I did it and I kind of liked it. It was fun and daring. I remember using all sorts of tricks to make the smoke go up, not under the door. Although it made me feel dizzy, for some reason I began to think it was sophisticated. Over the summer, I worked at a resort where I experimented a lot with smoking.

We'd smoke at parties and get a real high just from smoking tobacco cigarettes. I loved the dizziness. I can remember walking up the stairs and feeling giddy. I loved the feeling. I quickly became hooked, and I didn't even consider not smoking for probably the next fifteen years. I was a heavy smoker, smoking two to three packs a day depending on whether I was drinking or what I was doing at the time. And I liked every minute of smoking. For years, I loved the feeling, even when I had a cold.

My ex-husband smoked, and most of the people that I dated or who were my friends smoked. Nobody ever questioned smoking then.

However, over time, I developed a cough that persisted. I couldn't get rid of it. So at about age thirty-five, I quit for the first time. I signed up with a friend for a Seventh Day Adventist lecture designed to help you quit smoking. My friend didn't go to the lecture, but I went anyway. One of the things they recommended was eating oranges and prunes. I immediately ate a whole bag of oranges and a whole box of prunes. I got violently ill and could neither smoke nor get out of bed for three days. The experience did however take away my desire to smoke, and I was off cigarettes for six months.

During those six months, I loved not smoking. My cough went away, and I felt much healthier. I also had a lot more energy. But one day a friend came over, and she had a cigarette. I just wanted to taste it. I took one puff, and that was all it took to get me started once more. I was incredibly ashamed of starting again. I kept my smoking hidden from others for about a week. Then I had to let them know that I was doing it, because I couldn't stop smoking. I smoked again for about a year, all that time wanting not to smoke. I just couldn't ever get to that point of thinking of not smoking again. Then I developed a cold that was so severe I could not smoke. That helped me over the hump, and I quit again for about four months. Not smoking was actually easy after making it through the first three days. Once again, I felt really good. I didn't gain weight, and I had tons of energy. Most of my friends continued to smoke so I didn't have that many people supporting me in not smoking, but I didn't seem to need that.

Then I went through a crisis with a friend who had also quit smoking. There had been a death, and we had to arrange the funeral. The experience of doing that so unnerved me. I felt like I wasn't able to handle it. Because of the stress, my friend started to smoke again, and I decided I would just smoke cigars for a time and then quit after the time period had passed. I was sure I could break that off. I knew if I had a cigarette I'd go right back to full-time smoking. I smoked little cigars and big ones. I smoked at work. My coworkers thought it was strange, but I didn't care. I smoked wherever I was, inhaling all the time. My lungs began to really hurt, but I loved cigars. Then I started to become afraid. I'd heard that if you inhaled cigars, it was really dangerous, and I was inhaling and couldn't stop. Naturally, I went back to smoking cigarettes rather than continuing to endanger my health with cigars. I loved smoking from that moment on. I absolutely loved it, but I felt guilty about doing it. What I began to feel the guiltiest about was the damage I was doing to other people.

I remember smoking around an asthmatic. I had to talk to her from another room, talk around corners to her, knowing that I couldn't quit. Friends began telling me how much my smoking bothered them. they told me my house smelled awful from the smoke, and I began to feel embarrassed. I was also beginning to have some severe consequences. Another friend and I set a house on fire accidentally while smoking, and still I didn't quit. On a later occasion, I actually managed to set my own hair on fire. The money I was spending on my habit really bothered me as well. Yet I didn't quit again for another seven years.

When I thought I was ready to quit, I made an appointment with a hypnotist. I'd known others who had quit this way. I had to make the appointment weeks ahead. When the time came for my appointment, I cancelled it and just felt really bad. I just didn't have the strength to go through with it.

One day six months later, while driving to work on really icy streets, I started to hyperventilate. I was really scared and noticed that the cigarettes were making me even more afraid. That was the first time I had ever realized that smoking made me nervous. It did not calm me down as I'd always thought. I decided that I would never smoke again while driving when it was icy. That decision felt good, so I decided to take it one step further and never smoke in the car.

On that same icy day, I read my horoscope, and it said that whatever I started would be successful. I decided that I didn't want to go through a heavy withdrawal from smoking. I would just cut back and see if I could do that. I only smoked one cigarette every hour that day. The next day, I smoked one every two hours, but that's all I could think about. After about a week, I'd gotten down to two cigarettes a day. I was literally climbing the walls. I didn't know what to do. I had a friend who was quitting at the same time, so I called her and we talked and talked. That helped a lot. I think it is really important to find somebody who has quit smoking and knows what it's like, because that first week, I really, really wanted to smoke. I felt incredibly off-the-wall. The only place where I had never ever smoked was in my bed. So when I wasn't going to work or to a party with friends, I'd go home and jump in bed. That phase lasted about a week.

I was still struggling, and a friend suggested that I think of myself as a nonsmoker rather than as a smoker who had quit. Doing that was a real help. Another thing that helped at that time was envisioning myself in heaven heading for the smoking section. It helped me to think I would eventually be able to smoke again, even though not in this life.

Unlike the previous time when I'd quit, this time I did not feel physically good. I got colds, and since I was feeling deprived, I rewarded myself with sugar. Rewards are important. The first time I quit, I rewarded myself by buying jewelry with the money I saved by not smoking. This time, I craved desserts and rewarded myself with them. Even after eating a big meal, I never felt full that first year after quitting smoking. I was hungry all the time. After a while, I finally had the strength to quit the desserts, but not before I'd gained twenty-five pounds. I felt heavy and unattractive, and my clothes didn't fit. Physically I didn't feel any better from not smoking, and emotionally I was a wreck. I almost lost my job because my emotions were so crazy that I created a scene at work and got into big trouble. I didn't understand what I was doing. I felt out of control. The consequences of not smoking were very rough for a while, but I didn't want to go back to smoking. I didn't want to be addicted to anything.

I was particularly upset about the weight I gained, but a friend assured me I would lose it eventually, and I trusted that. By one year after quitting, I had lost part of the weight, and after another year, I took off the rest of it without needing to go on a diet. I thought it was very important to go through the struggle regardless of the pain. I had been using smoking to cover

Stop Smoking and Vaping Now!

up my emotions. I came to understand that if I wanted to know who I was, I had to forge ahead even though it was painful—*very* painful.

Today I do know myself and like myself much better. Prior to quitting, if I was upset about something, I would smoke rather than deal with it. Now I've learned that I have to deal with the issues that surface. Maybe it means accepting some anger and trying to work it out in some constructive way—or at least means admitting that I'm angry. I know now I have to do something other than sit on my feelings.

I haven't smoked now for five years, but every once in a while, especially if I'm doing something that I used to do while smoking, I'll want a cigarette. A couple of years ago, I went fishing, and the whole time we were out on the water I wanted to smoke. I had not fished since quitting smoking, and the two were very connected in my mind. Sometimes the urge is incredibly overwhelming. It just feels like I can't stand not smoking for one minute more. But the urge lasts for no more than a minute and then goes away. I don't generally know why the urge is occurring, but usually assume something from the past triggered it. Cravings come less frequently now; in fact, these days I can go without thinking about smoking for months on end.

What's been best about not smoking is that I'm more in touch with myself, and I love the freedom of being a nonsmoker. I don't have to constantly check whether I have enough cigarettes or where the lighter or matches are. I no longer wake up in the middle of the night and have to smoke a cigarette before I can get back to sleep. Now I never have to make sure I'll be able to make it through a whole movie without smoking. I'm beginning to feel better now as far as my health is concerned. Mentally I feel different too. Not needing to smoke gives me more time to myself. At first that was really hard for me. For instance, I couldn't just sit down and watch it snow. I had to keep moving. Now I am able to move around if I choose, but it's in a different way. I'm *watching* the snow; I'm not just sitting there smoking. I'm much more in touch with what's around me.

What I learned was that to become a happy nonsmoker, it helps to think of myself as one. It's not easy at first, but it is possible. Getting support from others, particularly supportive groups, was crucial; but if I could do it all over again, I wouldn't eat sweets. Taking in all that sugar gained me nothing but some extra pounds I had to lose.

"MY DRINKING TRIGGERED MY SMOKING EVERY TIME"

Robyn's Story

Robyn is a thirty-three-year-old professional dog groomer who owns her own business. She is enthusiastic about classic cars and loves gardening, animals, boating, and physical fitness, a pursuit she shares with her firefighter husband.

At fifteen, I experimented with maybe one or two cigarettes in a friend's basement, and I didn't like smoking. But at sixteen my friends and I started running around. We had our driver's licenses, so we'd go out for an evening of socializing and buy a pack of cigarettes to take along. We'd all buy cigarettes, and it was fun. Early on I limited my smoking to special occasions. But within a short time, I was smoking, along with drinking, every weekend. The fact that I was only a teenager didn't deter me. My mom and dad no longer smoked, and they were terribly against smoking, so I didn't want them to know I had started. When I moved out of the house at age seventeen or eighteen, I became an everyday smoker.

I became really hooked on cigarettes right away. Smoking was a big part of my life, and I loved it. Occasionally I'd smoke a cigarette and it wouldn't taste good, but not very often. Most of the time it tasted wonderful. I smoked a lot when I was nervous or sad. Cigarettes were my best friend. They were there with me all the time. They never deserted me. But I saw how they controlled me. I wasn't free to run into town to go to the store or go to get gas without first finding my cigarettes and my lighter and putting them in my purse. I didn't like that, but I kept puffing away.

Drinking and smoking paired up in my life. I smoked a lot when I drank. I normally smoked a pack and a half of cigarettes a day if I wasn't drinking and didn't go out in the evening. But when I went out and partied, I would smoke a pack of cigarettes in two or three hours. Drinking usually increased my smoking. The morning after, I would wake up and my lungs would feel awful. I think smoking a lot of cigarettes contributes to an alcohol hangover and makes it worse.

On a number of occasions, I wanted to quit smoking, and I tried. The first time I quit was about ten years ago, at age twenty-two. I started to worry about my health. I knew that if I smoked long enough, cigarettes would kill me. All smokers—*everybody*—knows that cigarettes are going to kill them. But for years I was just so addicted that I didn't think about it. I'd put it out of my mind and smoke anyway. My first husband, who was many years older, smoked three or four packs of cigarettes a day. Our house was a smoke factory. He perpetually smelled like a cigarette, and he had one with him constantly. I didn't want to end up like that. I was afraid if I kept on with my tobacco habit, I would end up smoking as many cigarettes per day as he did, so I quit. I did not smoke for a full year.

Even though my husband kept on smoking himself, he was very supportive of my not smoking. I needed that. When I really felt like having a cigarette, he'd say, "Oh, don't. I know you really want to quit. If you smoke it, you'll be sorry." His support helped a lot. Mom and Dad were really supportive too, because they had quit and wanted me to quit as well. I worried about putting on weight, and the first time I quit, I gained about ten pounds. I still felt good about quitting, though.

I went back to smoking when my marriage began to fall apart. I started to drink more, and my inhibitions were gone. One evening, I picked up a cigarette, thinking I would just smoke when I drank. And that's how it started. Every time I drank, I'd smoke, and for a while, that was enough. However, it was not long before I was getting up in the morning wanting a cup of coffee and a cigarette. I gave in to the desire very soon, and in no time was smoking more than I had smoked before I quit.

I continued to smoke another seven years but then quit for three months. I had remarried, and my husband's niece moved in with us. She and I drank a lot together. She smoked, too, and before long I started smoking when I was drinking. Soon I was right back to heavy smoking. I hadn't given not smoking a chance.

The next time I quit, my husband and I were getting ready to go on vacation. He quit, but he didn't tell me that he had quit. One day I noticed he wasn't smoking. I was really excited that he'd quit because I wanted to also. However, he wanted me to wait a month before I quit so he could get on a solid footing with it first. He feared we would really get on each other's nerves due to our tension over not smoking. So I waited the month, and then I quit. We went on vacation free of smoking—but I relapsed within six weeks. My drinking really triggered it. In fact, my drinking triggered it every time. I'd be okay until I got a beer or a shot of liquor in my hand, and then I'd want a cigarette.

Quitting feels different this time. I really want to take control of my life. Drinking was controlling me. Nicotine was controlling me. I decided that the only way I was going to be able to quit smoking was to quit drinking too. I don't know that I really thought of myself as an alcoholic initially, but I decided the only way for me to quit drinking and feel good about it was to go to Alcoholics Anonymous. I went to a meeting and discovered that in fact, I was an alcoholic.

I am an alcoholic. I have alcoholic drinking tendencies, and if I keep drinking, I will end up in very serious trouble with alcohol. So I quit drinking five weeks ago. At first, I thought maybe I should wait a little longer before I quit smoking, but I feel so good about not drinking that I feel strong enough to tackle my tobacco problem too. I quit smoking ten days ago by going to a free stop-smoking clinic at the hospital.

There were probably twenty-five people who went to the first meeting. There was a group leader, and it was very informal. It was similar to an A.A. meeting in that everybody introduced themselves and said a little about their smoking habit, why they wanted to quit, and if they had tried to quit before. The leader explained the program, which included setting a quit date. We talked about cigarettes being our best friend and how difficult it is to quit smoking. Many of us shared our worries about gaining weight.

There were four meetings, one a week for a month, and they each lasted about two hours. Originally I set my quit date for a week after the first meeting. However, I had a bad cold at the time of the first meeting, and I went home after attending and coughed all night long. I thought, "This is stupid. Why am I waiting a week to quit smoking?" I really wanted to quit. I had made up my mind that I wanted to quit. So I decided to quit immediately. I woke up the next morning and used what I had learned in A.A. about asking my Higher Power for help. My desire to smoke was taken away there and then. Every time I wanted a cigarette, which was quite often those first few days, I asked the Higher Power to take the desire to smoke away. And it was gone! I know it helped that I had made up my mind to quit.

I still have the cough because I'm still getting over that cold, but it's getting better. I'm coughing up a lot of phlegm, but the doctor at the smokers' meeting said that it's helping to clear the lungs faster. He advised us to breathe deeply and do lung exercises. He told us the lungs do recover in most cases. Unless you've smoked for forty or fifty years, you'll recover almost 100 percent providing you have not contracted COPD or some other serious disease.

Many wonderful things are happening to me as a nonsmoker, and I think a lot of it has to do with the A.A. program. I'm getting in touch with myself and my real feelings and letting them be known. Before, I never did. I drank and smoked and just hid from myself inside myself. I am getting in touch with why I feel the way I do about certain things, and I'm talking to myself and other people about this. before, when I wasn't drinking, I would smoke if I felt down. I would not think about things. I'd just smoke cigarettes. But now the feelings are present.

Sometimes my feelings frighten me a little bit, but physically I feel much better. I *smell* better. In fact, everything smells better. Food smells better and it tastes better, too, which is kind of scary since I am experiencing that oral longing for something in my mouth to satisfy the cravings I used to fill with smoking. Food seems like the obvious and natural substitute, but I made up my mind that I was not going to gain weight when I quit. I don't really feel hungrier than I used to except that when I felt these hunger feelings before, I covered them up with cigarettes. If I really didn't want to eat, I'd light up a cigarette and smoke and drink a Coke or something. now I've made up my mind that if I eat something, it's going to be non-fattening, perhaps carrot or celery sticks.

I chewed a lot of gum those first few days off of cigarettes. I don't much care for gum, however. I've used Certs and other breath mints. If I'm in a certain situation where I know I would have smoked in the past, I'm removing myself from that situation. for instance, after dinner, instead of sitting at the supper table and smoking a cigarette with my husband, I get up and clear the table right away and start on the dishes. Otherwise it's too painful for me to sit there and watch him smoke a cigarette. Rather than sitting there eating another helping while he's smoking a cigarette, I just get up. I think that eventually I won't have to do that, but right now quitting is still too new and I do have to take precautions. One exceptional reward from not smoking is that I can sleep a half hour longer in the morning. I don't have to have time for coffee, cigarettes, and the paper. I don't through the daily newspaper in the morning anymore, but I know I'd be feeling deprived if I couldn't have a cigarette while drinking my coffee and reading the paper, so I'm just not placing myself in that situation. I am changing my patterns, and I'm taking control. The nicotine is no longer in control, and that feels good. I feel really good. I've never been in control of cigarettes before, and now I am.

So many things have changed in such a short time. I was feeling really bad about my work situation; there were a lot of things that needed to be dealt with there, and I was not dealing with them. I was letting my whole life slip by me, not taking control of it, instead passively thinking that that's just the way life is. I drank and I smoked and I just put up with things. I'm finding out life is what you make it. Life is exciting when I take charge and do what I want. I've always heard people say you can do whatever you want. I've always heard that. My dad always told me that I could be whatever I wanted if I put my mind to it—I never believed it then, but it's true. And I'm learning now that I can do whatever I want with my life. If I can quit smoking, I can do anything. Quitting smoking and quitting drinking are just the first steps for me. I feel excited about my future at last.

It's funny. I never expected to be saying these things. I had watched my grandmother die of lung cancer even though she'd quit smoking probably fifteen years earlier. She discovered she had lung cancer six months after she retired. They removed a lung, but it had already gone into the lymph glands, and then it recurred elsewhere. She died a horrible, horrible death, a miserable death. I watched her die, and I smoked the whole time. That's part of the denial of cigarettes. I was so hooked on them that I just denied that it could happen to me.

I was able to watch her die and still smoke. I can't believe I did that. Her death really did affect me, and I kept thinking, I've got to quit, I've got to quit, but I put it off and put it off. Finally, over a year later, I'm doing something about it.

To handle the oral fixation, I eat carrot sticks; I bring what you might call "rabbit food" to work: broccoli, cauliflower, a dip, and maybe a banana—things that I really enjoy eating that take time to eat. I'm satisfying my hunger, and I'm not putting on weight. I'm doing healthy things for myself. I'm eating food that really is good for me, and the health aspect of it is really exciting. I'm doing good things for my body, and my body feels better. I'm really into being healthy now when I never was before. I'd always thought people who jogged and did all that crap were weird. But you know, now I'm exercising too! Getting healthy is exciting; it's fun, and the future excites me.

Joyce's Story

Joyce, age fifty-one, a divorced mother of four, is a sorority house mother who is herself finishing a liberal arts degree at a major university. She is a talented tennis player who has discovered a love for art history.

I first smoked cigarettes while still in junior high, in what the kids in my neighborhood called "the back field." But I didn't smoke regularly until age sixteen. I was out with a boyfriend, and we were on some swings on a porch. He smoked Lucky Strikes, and he asked me if I wanted one. I took one and knew right away that cigarette was more serious than the 'back field cigarettes.' It made me dizzy, and I felt that between the swinging and the cigarette, I was going to get sick. But I had no thought of not doing it again. I believed smoking was something to get used to. My father and mother both smoked. However, I always felt disdainful of the way my mother smoked. She didn't inhale, and I always thought she looked dumb. I snuck cigarettes from my dad's pack because I didn't have much money.

Sometime during that period when I was sixteen to eighteen years old, I got hooked. I recall experiencing a car accident when I was about sixteen or seventeen, and immediately after the crash, my first thought was, where are my cigarettes? I knew even then that it was a very strange thing to wonder because I'd almost been killed.

I think I was hooked on nicotine almost right away. In my family, I was forbidden to smoke in front of anyone until I was seventeen, so on my seventeenth birthday, I lit up at the dining room table just like my parents. What a rite of passage that was. It really was the sign that I had become an adult.

I thought smoking was sexy and glamorous, and it was wonderful to be out on a date and have the boy do like Humphrey Bogart and put two cigarettes in his mouth and light them with one match. For years I thought of cigarettes as my best friend. I loved smoking. I smoked first thing in the morning and last thing at night, and a whole lot in between. My children hated it. I have four children, and I can remember how every time we would get in the car and I would light up, they would start coughing and fanning the air. I would get so angry at them.

For thirty-two years I smoked. That's a lot of cigarettes at three packs a day, and a lot of money. During those thirty-two years I tried to quit a couple of times. Once, about ten years before I successfully quit, I went to an American Cancer Society no-smoking clinic and made it through five days of not smoking. I had started getting a little scared because of the surgeon general's report. I knew cancer could happen, but in reality, I didn't think it would happen to me. but just in case, I thought I'd quit. It didn't work. Those five days were terrible. I felt like I'd lost my best friend, and I didn't know how to cope with the grief of that. I had no coping skills at all. The doctor told me to take more Valium until I was over the hump.

A few years later, I tried to quit another time on my own. I created a little tool to help myself: I made a bracelet out of a piece of leather with twenty colored beads. Every time that I didn't smoke a cigarette during the day, I moved one of the beads around. I made it about the same length of time as on my first attempt, five days. I remember coming home from work and throwing myself on my bed, saying, "What's the use? I don't even want to live if I can't smoke." I cried a whole lot, and then I had a cigarette. I felt better immediately.

For a year or two before I successfully quit, I smoked the long brown cigarettes. I was working as a secretary, and every time I would type anything, the cigarette would go out in the ashtray, and I'd have to light it again, sometimes as many as ten times. I'm not sure if relighting the stale cigarettes caused it or something else, but I started to develop a really bad cough. I got a cold, and then it turned into bronchitis. Even when the cold was gone, I kept on coughing. It went on for weeks and weeks. People at work could hear me coughing. It was embarrassing to me even right after I'd get through one of those coughing spells, then I'd light up a cigarette. It seemed so abusive to myself, but I was addicted. Also, by then I had been sober for a while and I'd learned what it meant to be abusive to myself. It was beginning to be clear to me that there was something wrong with the way I was living my life.

The cough kept up for quite a while, and I was really scared because it wouldn't go away. I could understand coughing while I had the cold, but it worried me how it lingered and lingered and lingered. Friends began expressing concern about my cough. It was very deep, and I was scared.

One by one, the other women where I worked had been giving up smoking. There were maybe six of us left out of twenty-three who were still puffing away. I was beginning to get annoyed that I was singled out as a smoker at restaurants; it always seemed to take longer to get seated. I was starting to feel a gap opening between myself and nonsmokers, and I felt defensive and ashamed.

What helped me most when I finally quit smoking was having gone through a really difficult recovery from alcohol and other drugs and then through an absolutely brutal divorce. I realized

Stop Smoking and Vaping Now!

that although I had survived the worst pain I had ever experienced in my life, I was going to kill myself with cigarettes. It didn't make any sense to me, and it made me really angry. I used to say, "I didn't go through all this pain to kill myself with a cigarette now!" That's where my resolve came from. I'd already lived through a couple of experiences that nearly felt like dying, and I figured I could make it through one more.

I didn't realize how effective the steps I took to quit were going to be, but I started doing some visual imagery work where I pictured myself as a nonsmoker in advance of actually becoming one. I had a tape about goal setting, and it talked about using visualization. It suggested making a scrapbook of my goals so that they would be tangible; that way I could look at them and start to realize them in my head. I cut out a picture of a woman smoking a brown cigarette, the same as the ones I smoked. Then I found a picture of a big red stop sign. I pasted the stop sign on top of the woman smoking. I also cut out some other pictures of a car I wanted and a house and a man as well. I began visualizing the picture of the woman a lot. The image would just come to me. Apparently that helped, because the day I quit smoking, I had no plans to quit at all. I hadn't made a date yet. I was coming home at ten o'clock in the morning, and I was smoking the very last cigarette in my pack. It was a very cold January day, and for the first time in my life, I just didn't feel like stopping for a pack of cigarettes. I knew a friend of mine who smoked was coming over, and I figured I could wait an hour until she got there—which was a pretty unusual thought for me.

I finished that cigarette and waited for my friend to come. It turned out that she didn't get there in an hour; she got there in an hour and a half, by which time I was pretty anxious. When she got there, she didn't have any cigarettes either. We talked about taking a walk around the lake and decided to try the walk without a cigarette, both of us. by this time, she was getting interested in how long I had been without a cigarette. We walked around the lake, and by then it was probably two and a half to three hours without a cigarette, and I decided to keep going. Since I'd made it three hours, I figured I could make it a little bit longer. I've never had a cigarette since.

It was awful at first—I didn't like it at all. That first night, I went out to dinner, and it felt like I was taking one of the greatest pleasures away from myself. I can remember sitting in that Chinese restaurant when I was all done eating, drinking some tea. I felt pretty cheated. But still, I realized that I'd gone through half a day and I hadn't come apart at the seams, so I decided to keep going with it.

When things got really hard in my life, friends suggested I work A.A.'s Twelve Steps, but that didn't work for me. The thing that made the most sense to me was that I had gone through so much in my life to be a healthy, strong woman, and I didn't want to kill myself anymore with alcohol and other drugs, bad relationships, or cigarettes. My resolve was very strong. I kept using imagery, seeing that woman in my mind. I can see her still. I was strongly tempted two weeks after I'd quit smoking. I had a major crisis, and I went out and bought a pack of cigarettes. I bought Barkley brand, which I'd never smoked in my life. I knew someone who was trying to quit smoking, and he smoked Barkleys. It made perfect sense to me, since they have a lot less tar and nicotine. I didn't ever unwrap that pack, as it turned out.

I met a friend at the movies that afternoon. She was my coworker and knew that I had just quit smoking. I met her in the lobby at the movie and confessed that I'd just bought some cigarettes. She put her hand out and said, "Want to give them to me?" I did. After the movie, I said good-bye to her, then went to a store and bought four candy bars—I ate them all the way to another friend's house.

I began eating a whole lot of food that had sugar in it, and I put on twenty pounds in two and a half weeks. I really substituted one craving for another. But I still felt that as long as I wasn't smoking, I'd worry about taking the weight off later. I knew if I weakened on quitting tobacco because of gaining weight and went back to smoking, I'd be caught forever. I would always have that excuse then. But I never smoked, even though I hated gaining the weight. My body image was very important to me, and all the extra pounds did cause me a lot of pain. I kept all the extra weight for over three years, but I didn't smoke.

During my withdrawal, I felt like a robot. Even my lips felt numb. I didn't feel really emotional because I kept eating lots of ice cream and other sweets. Eating kept me in a state of "drunkenness" or "nicotine-ness." I was truly in a daze and actually walked into a couple walls. I was really out of it. I would forget why I was having such a hard time or why I seemed to be so dazed. Friends reminded me that I'd just quit smoking. It didn't make sense to me, but I did trust their reminders that I was going through withdrawal. After about six weeks, I went to a chiropractor who recommended a lot of vitamins, particularly vitamin C. Vitamin C helped get rid of some of the toxins in my system. He promised I'd already lived through the worst of it, and I started taking a lot of vitamin C.

I began feeling very proud that I had quit smoking. Having my cough go away almost immediately was a great benefit, and the freedom of not having to check every minute if I had cigarettes and a lighter or matches and everything that I used to need to carry around with me was the best of all. I never carried just one pack; I carried two packs in case I smoked all of the first pack. The feeling of freedom was great. It made me happy to see how thrilled my children were that I was now a nonsmoker.

I've really struggled with the weight gain, to the point that I even considered smoking again, but I know what addiction is, and I know that if I even smoke one cigarette, I may not be able to give them up again. I know if I ever give in, I will be done. The hardest times for me are when I'm walking into the house where I reside in my position as sorority house mother and a see a single cigarette lying on the floor. I want to pick it up and smoke it. I don't know why. It's just that a cigarette in its purest state really tempts me.

For me, the best part of not smoking has been the knowledge that I'm no longer doing something that is abusive, unhealthy, and a dirty habit. I love myself enough to go through whatever is needed to be good to myself. I feel sad when I look at smokers, when I realize what they're doing to themselves and how hard it is for them to quit. I wish I could give them something to help them get off cigarettes. What I've noticed about women who smoke in particular is that their skin color is generally gray. They just look less healthy than nonsmokers.

I realize now that smoking smells awful. I didn't realize how bad I had smelled until I quit. My clothes smelled so dreadful. My kids used to tell me that, but I didn't believe them because I couldn't smell anything. After I stopped smoking, I couldn't believe how bad my closet smelled. It was like a heavily used ashtray.

As I look back on my life, I realize that in order to stay sober, I had to get out of my marriage, and I guess I thought if I could leave that marriage, with all the pain that entailed, then I could quit smoking. Now I'm into physical fitness. I can feel the difference when I don't exercise. I begin to notice feelings of lethargy or depression settling in if I don't get enough exercise.

The most important thing I realized in the process of quitting smoking was that it wasn't as hard as I had expected. It was all the negative self-talk prior to quitting that had me convinced that I couldn't make it. There are a lot of other things that I have done in the past eight years that were much harder and much more painful than quitting smoking.

———————

Matt's Story

Matt, age forty-five, is a retired commercial airline pilot. Married with no children,
he works full-time as a hobbyist building vintage cars, cabins, and furniture for his and his
wife's personal use.

I started smoking leaves when I was about nine years old. In the fall, we would take the leaves that fell off the oak trees and roll them up in newspapers to make cigars. We'd wet the leaves down and roll them up in our hands to get them into small pieces. Then we'd roll them in a dampened newspaper. They would actually look like cigars, and because I was really good with my hands, I got to be the best cigar maker in the neighborhood. I used to have a cigar box full of leaf and newspaper cigars, and all the boys would come to my tent, and we would smoke those every fall. It was a tradition that lasted for two or three years, a wonderful fall ritual.

When I started high school, due to peer pressure, I started smoking real cigarettes with a bunch of kids I rode to school with. At about age sixteen or seventeen, my folks said, "If you're going to smoke, you might as well smoke at home." So I started smoking at home while I was in high school. My folks never discussed whether smoking was good or bad. It was a grown-up's habit. My parents had always said it would stunt a person's growth. I don't know where that notion came from, but it was a popular one when I was growing up.

I was used to being around smokers. My dad was a moderate to heavy smoker; my mom was more light to moderate, and all of my aunts and uncles as well as all my adult cousins smoked. Anyone who didn't smoke was the exception in my family.

I loved smoking when I was a young kid. It made me feel grown-up. It made me feel like I'd reached manhood or adulthood because only adults could do it. I had the feeling of being accepted. The only two things that made me feel really accepted as an adult by my parents were when they said I could drive the car and when they allowed me to smoke cigarettes in the house. Smoking was a major rite of passage into adulthood. I even liked the yellow stains on my fingers. They were some kind of badge or mark of status to me. They proved I wasn't smoking Kents; a real man smoked Camels or Luckys. In my mind at that time, there were real men's cigarettes and then there were women's cigarettes. I would smoke three or four Camels and let them burn down onto my hand until it hurt. That made my fingers dark brown. I can remember a friend's dad who was a welder and a real tough guy. He had serious brown stains between the first and second fingers on his hand. That impressed me. He was a real man. The smell, the taste, and the burns all seemed attractive to me then.

I went into the Navy out of high school, and there it was like standard procedure to smoke. There were designated times and places where we could smoke, and they just automatically assumed (and joked) that the only reason you wouldn't smoke is that you were not in a properly designated area. During my military years, I smoked maybe a pack a day. I probably stayed at a pack a day for the next five years.

Right about the time when the US Surgeon General informed the public that smoking was not good for us, I started flying airplanes. I was involved with a different group of people than in the military or in college. These people were more concerned about their health status and their ability to pass medical exams every six months. I was getting the message that smoking was not healthy. I was starting to fly and going to moderately high altitudes—15,000 to 18,000 feet. I was flying in the mountains and doing work with the Forest Service without oxygen on board, and I was getting dull headaches. I talked to several people about it and deduced that my headaches were caused by the smoking. I'd go up in altitude for three hours at 15,000 or 16,000 feet, smoke half-a-dozen cigarettes, and come down with a dull headache. I believed it was from oxygen starvation, so I started chewing tobacco instead and developed a fairly strong habit almost immediately.

I went from cigarettes to whole leaf chewing tobacco, and within months, I was a serious Copenhagen user. I found that by chewing, I could get my nicotine fix not only more easily and stronger, but I could make it steady, all the time, even when my hands were busy. When I smoked, I couldn't feed my nicotine habit when I was busy using my hands. I immediately became really interested in chewing and increased the amount I was chewing and how much I chewed at a time. I didn't spit. I swallowed the nicotine. I felt spitting was pretty socially unacceptable, so I swallowed the saliva. I figured real men did it that way. Only the wimps spit out the juice. Of course, that meant I was not only taking that much nicotine in my mouth, but in my stomach too. I was getting very heavy doses of nicotine, and I developed a heavy habit that lasted twenty years or so.

I became more conscious of the health risks, and because I had to take a medical test every year, I realized that if I wanted to pass the exams, smoking was not a good deal. It was harmful. For twenty years, I knew I shouldn't be doing tobacco of any kind. However, I believed that smoking was more harmful than chewing. I was deluded about Copenhagen. For ten or twelve years, I pretended that Copenhagen wasn't that harmful because it wasn't damaging my lungs.

During my early years on Copenhagen, not too much was known about its health consequences. But about ten years ago, I started hearing things about mouth cancer. The mouth is a very efficient organ for ingesting a substance. Sucking on Copenhagen meant taking it directly into my bloodstream. I gradually became more aware of the damage I was doing, and I started suffering from headaches, too. I felt like there was a connection between my headaches and the nicotine poison in my body.

For about ten years, I tried to quit Copenhagen. But when I didn't have a can of nicotine, I smoked cigarettes if they were available. At times I would even do both. Sometimes I would have Copenhagen in my mouth, and if we were sitting around the table drinking coffee and someone was smoking a cigarette, I would smoke a cigarette too because it was fun to do. But as cigarettes became less socially unacceptable, I quit smoking them altogether. I felt like anybody who still used cigarettes in public was really thought of as a fool. I looked down on people who did that as weak and foolish. My tobacco use was not a public thing, and if someone caught me smoking cigarettes, I felt embarrassed.

I have a whole history of quitting. I would quit doing tobacco altogether, everything; no cigarettes, no chewing tobacco of any sort. I'd put on ten or twelve pounds within a period of six months or less because of my oral fixation. I would suck on lots of candy and eat lots of desserts and too much food in general. I knew I could lose the weight immediately if I started chewing tobacco again, so I would, automatically and deliberately. I did that many times over a period of ten years. Yet I was still in a lot of denial. I didn't consciously feel like I was committing suicide on the installment plan. I deliberately denied that there was any problem with my tobacco use. I could quit anytime! I'd prove it! I would just do it for a few days or a few weeks. It was not going to be a big problem. And then every once in a while, reality would hit me in the face. I'd look back and realize I'd been consuming tobacco again for three or four years.

I got into recovery from alcoholism, and the treatment process taught me how to confront reality. I started looking at the issue of my tobacco use and knew I shouldn't be doing it. I knew I was killing myself and that when I kept on doing it, I'd hate myself. The only way to live with myself was to either quit or deny, and I did one or the other for ten years.

I began to really get in trouble with my own values. I would quit, but then would become a closet user so my wife wouldn't know. I would hide my supply. I could do that for up to six months before she caught me. And it was really painful. I was embarrassed and ashamed because I knew that I didn't want to do it. I knew that I had either implied or directly told her that I didn't want her to help me. So when I was doing it, I knew that she would be very disappointed. It was really shameful.

Quitting feels different this last time. My dad came down with cancer of the throat. He was a heavy smoker for fifty years, and then got cancer of the throat at age seventy-five. It started with just a cough he couldn't get rid of. He went to see his doctor, but by the time they had diagnosed his condition, it had become necessary to take out his larynx. They were able to salvage enough of his voice box so that he could kind of make himself understood, but going through that whole process with him shook me. Being there at the hospital almost every day for weeks on end and seeing all these people at the hospital with their voice boxes gone really got to me. The guy in the bed next to my dad was a Copenhagen smokeless tobacco user, and he'd had part of his chin cut off and his lower jaw cut away. They grafted a bone from his leg onto his face as part of the reconstruction.

That experience really forced me to confront the issue of heredity and my own tobacco use as a form of slow suicide–all the things that I'd been denying for years. I came to the realization that I don't have the choice anymore of continuing to do it. I can't choose it anymore. My belief in heredity is strong enough that I don't have that option of using tobacco any longer. I'm confronted with facts about heredity that I believe are real.

Each time I quit, my process has been to do it on a date that has a meaningful connection. I've used the first of January, or my birthday, or Labor Day. I believed that I needed a date to quit that had significance to me. This last time, I quit on my sister's and mother's birthday, the thirteenth of June.

The first two weeks, I went into a rage on two separate occasions. Once I was with one of my very best friends, and it was over something totally insignificant. As far as our relationship was concerned, it was totally pointless and needless. Yet I flew into a rage that went on for days. About a week or ten days later, I saw him again, and as we tried to discuss it, I flew into another rage that went on for several hours. My wife helped me see how out of control I was with anger, and I began to connect the fact that I had been using tobacco to get me through periods of time when I needed to deal with my feelings. Rather than facing my inner emotions, instead I would take a hit of tobacco and stuff them down. I was using tobacco like a drug. Instead of saying, "I'm really feeling angry," I would just take a hit of tobacco and not do anything with the rage. I had a lot of rage over a whole bunch of things that I was stuffing. During that first couple weeks, my feelings were acutely apparent. I haven't had any rageful episodes since the first two weeks, and I've now got three or four months free of tobacco.

I was heavily addicted. I think cigarettes are pretty mild in comparison to Copenhagen [chewing tobacco]. The smoke from cigarettes is diluted with oxygen as you draw it in. There's only so much nicotine that can be absorbed, even if you're a chain-smoker using sixteen or eighteen hours a day. I was getting more nicotine in my blood by not spitting and by having tobacco in my mouth every single waking moment of the day, except during those three meals of fifteen minutes or whatever they were. Sometimes I even slept with Copenhagen in my mouth so I kept getting a good supply of nicotine into my bloodstream.

When I finally got off it, I had withdrawal sensations similar to what a person would experience getting off of heroin. I had an itchiness that felt like it was from within. I'd scratch, but it wouldn't relieve the itch. The itchiness was all over my entire body. It went on for four or five days and nights. I was most acutely aware of it at night. I would wake up every fifteen or twenty minutes and scratch all over my body; I'd scratch my head, shoulders, legs, chest, and torso. I'd itch from within, but I would scratch from without. I wouldn't be able to relieve the itching. It was a mildly uncomfortable itch that would keep me awake. Then I would fall back to sleep and wake up in twenty minutes and do it all over again.

To help me over my urges to use again, I used the Alcoholics Anonymous program of one day at a time. I don't have to quit forever; I can go back and use tobacco tomorrow if I want to. All I have to do is just not use it today. Someone asked me one day how many years I'd been using Copenhagen. I replied, "A few years, maybe five." But then I stopped and added it up, and it was twenty-one years. That's twenty-one years of one day at a time. It seemed like only five. So why couldn't the reverse be true? I could be off tobacco for twenty-one years, but it might seem like a couple years; or I could stay off it for a couple years, but it may seem like just a couple months. In other words, I can use that sensation of the shrinkage of time to my benefit. I don't have to quit forever, or for one year or five years or twenty. Just one day is all I have to quit for and they'll add up. Someday someone will say, "How long you been off cigarettes or off tobacco?" and I'll tell them, "Oh, I don't know, a few years." And I'll sit down and add it up and discover it's been twenty-one years.

As with the previous times when I'd quit, I feared putting on weight. So I made a decision to start exercising on a regular basis. Because I was aware I was getting on to mid-age, and because of my father's arthritic condition and my own symptoms of the onset of arthritis, I decided to begin a serious and regular exercise program. Again, I did not make the decision to do it forever, but just to do it for a short period of time. My commitment was that I would do it without question and without reneging on that promise. My initial promise to myself to exercise was for a period of six months. No matter what, I would do it for an hour three days a week, and then I would reassess. At that time, I would have a chance to see if I'd put on extra weight. And if I had, I would make another choice to either go back to tobacco or to increase my exercise or to decrease my caloric intake.

Since quitting, I've felt like I'm in a honeymoon period. I'm really positive. Physically I've felt really strong. The arthritis that used to bother me in the mornings hasn't been happening for the last couple months. I don't know if it's because of the exercise or the fact that I haven't got those tobacco poisons running through my bloodstream anymore—or both. I just feel a lot more positive, a lot better about myself.

I miss the tobacco. I think of it as a wonderful friend. It offered solace from pain. It was an awesome way to retreat from it. For years I had used drugs to hide from pain, whether emotional, physical, or mental. I still think of tobacco every day even though I'm happier not using it. But it's like any addiction. This is no different in my mind. Nicotine is a drug, and I'm an addictive personality. I look at the drug as one of my best friends, and I know that I'm only one cigarette away from being back to a two-pack-a-day user. But I can't afford the luxury of doing it. It's a friend that I know is really an enemy. It's one of my worst enemies—that I think of as a friend. This is the great paradox about the part that alcohol and other drugs play in people's lives. People think of drugs as friends because they can use them to retreat from their pain; they do this for many, many years and then all of a sudden find out they can't do it anymore. The 'friend' has turned into an enemy. That's how I think of tobacco.

That friend, after all those years, is now one of my worst enemies. He tried to kill me, and with that, I became conscious of the change in our friendship. I don't know why. I guess my own perception changed. Maybe it was a miracle. For many years, I was privy to all the facts about tobacco as a killer, but I still chose to deny those facts. I don't know why at this time I began to think of it as one of my worst enemies. I just know I don't have the luxury of being friends with tobacco because it will kill me if I do.

I grieve for smokers because I know there's nothing I can say or do that will stop them from smoking or vaping or chewing or whatever it is they do. I know they have to change in their own time and through their own process. All I can do is not smoke. Maybe my example will help someone else.

I've learned that a drug is a drug. It's suicide on the installment plan for an addictive personality like mine. No longer killing myself on an installment plan feels wonderful. I feel like I'm voting to live rather than voting to die. I'm enjoying life enough to want to stay alive for it. Even though that's how I feel, I still think about tobacco every day; but I just say to myself, "Don't do it today. Just chew some gum, or eat some candy—just don't do it today."

As the months and years go by, I know I'll think about it less often. But even if I never get over the urge, I just hope I can remember that all I've got to do is not do it for twenty more minutes. That's all I've got to worry about.

"FOR ME, SMOKING WAS
THE MANLY THING TO DO"

Terry's Story

Terry, age forty, is a professional writer and editor. Married and the father of two boys,
he loves humor, playing baseball, and the Chicago Cubs.

Neither I nor most of my friends in the early years smoked. They were either athletes or at least into athletics of some kind. It was obvious which ones did smoke. They were always short of wind.

It wasn't that we didn't smoke because of school rules around athletics, it was just how we played in grade school. When I reached high school, there were rules that no student was allowed to smoke, but of course anybody who wanted to did. And they did, all over the grounds. I did have some friends who smoked in high school, but it just never occurred to me to smoke.

I was slow in taking to smoking, and I didn't take to it much even when I was in college. I remember one occasion during my sophomore year when I was feeling really lost. I think I was in college more to please my folks than myself. I got into sitting up till all hours in the dorm rooms, talking with my buddies in all-night conversations—and one of them smoked. One night, I decided I'd try a cigarette and smoked a few Tareytons; they tasted awful. I thought, oh boy, how can anyone *do* this? My friend said, "Hey, that's okay. Don't judge it on one night, you'll get used to it." However, the next morning I went out and bought a pack of L & Ms instead.

I smoked a couple and noticed that they did funny things when you lit them. sometimes there'd be a little explosion on the end of the cigarette. One side would burn and the other side wouldn't. I thought, wow, what is this stuff? I tossed them, and I didn't smoke again until the next fall, when I bought a different kind. Even then, I bought cigarettes only once in a while. I might buy a pack on a Friday if I had money, and I'd smoke one every now and then until they were gone. It was usually an occasional thing. Smoking was a reward I indulged in if I finished a paper or maybe did well on a test.

In the spring of my junior year, I was again going through a period when I was very tense. I didn't know if I wanted to stay in school, and I started cutting class. At the same time, I ran out of money, so I wasn't smoking. I dropped out of school, and it took me a couple months to find a job. After I started working, I would have a cigarette every once in a while. There was something about smoking and taking a break. One of the people I worked with smoked, and he took a break in the morning and a break in the afternoon. I'd take cigarettes with me to work and leave them in my desk drawer, and then have a cigarette on break. And then at night, if I was going out, I would take two or three out of the pack to take along. But I still wasn't really into smoking. I don't think I was addicted to the nicotine, although I really liked the effect it had on me. I had realized on the first night that I smoked years earlier that after I had one, I didn't feel the next three or four that I had. I wasn't sure why that was the case, but smoking energized me. The nicotine made me tremble and it made me high.

Shortly thereafter, I joined the military. There was a lot going on in my life at that point, and I was not yet twenty-one. Before enlisting, I had still been smoking, but not much. Usually I just couldn't afford it. I could barely afford to live. At that time, my big indulgence was going down to Mr. Steak on Sunday afternoon, or sometimes I'd go for a pizza.

In basic training, we couldn't have anything—no personal possessions. The only thing we could buy was cigarettes. Everybody smoked, and so did I. I smoked nonfiltered cigarettes because if we smoked filters, we had to keep the leftover filters in our pockets when we were done with a cigarette. We couldn't just drop them on the ground. We had to "fieldstrip" all butts, which meant letting all the tobacco out, rolling the paper up in a tiny little ball, and then keeping that in our pockets. The idea was to keep the ground clean. This training was also to protect us in combat. If we were in combat and we camped someplace, nothing could be left behind that would leave a trace. The army was really strict about smoking.

After not smoking much for years, I was all of a sudden smoking unfiltered Pall Malls; and even today, I can't look at a pack of Pall Malls without thinking of basic training. That was the only time I ever smoked them. I must have smoked two or three cartons during basic training. There was nothing else to do, and it kept me occupied. It was a cheap activity; a pack of cigarettes was really cheap back then. It was better than going to the PX and drinking 3.2 percent beer. Smoking was something I could do. I would sit out on the fire escape feeling like the classic Hollywood actor Robert Taylor, who really knew how to smoke a cigarette. It was kind of dramatic to sit out there on the fire escape and light up with the sun going down. My real history with smoking started then, and I smoked all through my time in the army.

And then about a year after I got out of the military, I quit. I decided I just didn't want to smoke anymore. I had gotten married and gone back to school. The first year I was back in school, we were pretty poor. We lived on the GI Bill, which wasn't a lot of money. I wasn't eating enough, and my weight was down to about 155 pounds. I figured if I stopped smoking, we'd have more money for food. It was a really simple equation. So I quit, and immediately my taste buds came back. I started getting hungry, and I ate a lot more food. I was afraid I was going to get fat, so I started working out with weights and riding a bicycle everywhere. I did put on about twenty pounds, but it was good weight, more muscle than fat. And then about a year after I quit, my wife quit. Neither of us smoked for the rest of the time we were undergraduates at college in Illinois.

We went from there to the writers' program in Iowa City, Iowa. My wife moved to Iowa City before me because I had three weeks left to work, and we needed to save all the money we could. I moved her into our new apartment and then returned to Illinois and worked those last three weeks. When I got back to Iowa, she was smoking again. That bummed me out, but I didn't say anything. Almost two years later, I started bumming cigarettes from her once in a while. Occasionally I'd have a cigarette if I really felt like having one. And that seemed okay. It was a positive decision. But then I started smoking regularly again, and I was looking to feel the effects at that point. I wanted that sensation I'd had years before. Otherwise smoking was just a habit with no reward.

From then on, I smoked until I quit three years ago. There were some brief periods when I didn't smoke. During some summers I didn't because I was playing softball. I didn't want to carry cigarettes around with me, and I didn't want smoking to affect my wind and my endurance. Cigarettes were a lot of trouble. They'd spill out of the pack in my bag and be ruined and get tobacco all over. If I really wanted to have one, I could borrow one, but of course, nobody likes someone who does that too often. Finally, three years ago, I quit.

One of the things that encouraged me to quit was that I was sharing an office with a smoker and the room got awfully smoky, so smoky that even I didn't like it. D-Day came around and I thought I'd try not smoking. I figured I'd quit and get healthier. At the time, I was thinking a lot about changing my life, about quitting a lot of different things, like not playing kids' games anymore. I was nearly forty and figured I needed to spend more time doing yard work than playing softball. And I decided quitting smoking was another change I needed to make. So I did.

I didn't think about quitting ahead of time. I made no preparations for it. The first time that I had quit years earlier, somebody had suggested I smoke one less cigarette each day. and I figured, why bother? That just makes it harder because you think about it. I knew it would be easier for me to just stop.

That first day, I didn't have an urge to have a cigarette until after I ate lunch. And the craving lasted about half a minute. A friend had suggested I try lemon drops to satisfy the urge. I bought lemon drops and had one. I'd learned the first time I'd quit that nicotine affects the blood sugar and that without cigarettes, I craved sweets more, including soda. This time I got into yogurt, too, the kind with fruit. I quite literally replaced cigarettes with sugar for a while.

I didn't really have any physical withdrawal from smoking. I just had the craving that would come up once in a while. I also had a flat, dry feeling in my mouth. But a drink of water made it go away. Even though I haven't had a cigarette for three years, I do like to have a cigar on occasion. It's a ritual that has to do with my past. My grandpa smoked cigars when he'd sit around with the boys. So when my brother Dave and I sit around together, we'll have a cigar occasionally. Dave doesn't smoke cigarettes either.

Quitting was not physically difficult for me, but quitting any activity that rewards you means losing something from your life. During my earlier attempt at giving up the habit three years earlier, when I thought of smoking as an unpleasant activity, it was easy not to do it. but when I'd remember smoking in connection with enjoyable times, like sitting around after dinner with friends, then it was difficult. I knew something was missing. It wasn't the same to go get a lemon drop and rejoin the group at the dinner table. and it wasn't as romantic a feeling to sit around on the porch at sunset and suck on a lemon drop, so 'Robert Taylor' was gone.

I'm aware too that smoking provides something for the fingers to do. Often I wanted to have a cigarette because I was in a special situation where I didn't know what to do with my hands. With smoking, it's an automatic thing. You have an occupation for your hands. You move your hand from your mouth to the ashtray. It's rehearsed. There's a certain protocol. It's probably akin to the proper way one stood with hands in pockets in the eighteenth century.

As a smoker, these were things that were "preordained" for me to do with my hands. After quitting, there were times when I wished I had a cigarette, but I'd think about something else and drink a glass of water. I discovered a glass of water was a really good substitute because I'd hold it in my hand and move it to my mouth. It's almost the same kind of hand to mouth motion as with smoking, and it's good for you. I hardly ever drank water before that time even though I knew I needed lots of water every day. So for me, drinking water was cleansing. I used to visualize swallowing it and watching it travel through my system. It only took a little while to get over the urge to smoke. Even if I just thought about the cigarette for more than a minute, the sensation would go away. Even if I tried to keep that feeling, it would go away. I think something in the body happens to make you feel that, but if you don't give in to the craving, it just goes away.

I'm happy that I'm no longer satisfying those urges for a cigarette. I like not being dependent on cigarettes. However, smoking a cigar once in a while disqualifies me from being a total nonsmoker. Cigarettes are really hard to get out of your system. I do think there's an addiction at work, and maybe I've replaced it with something else. I'm not sure. But I am sure that living free of cigarettes gives me more energy. That's the number one benefit, having both more mental and physical energy. I have more willingness and more time to do other things. If a person smokes a pack a day and it takes seven minutes to smoke a cigarette, that's 140 minutes daily, which means almost two and a half hours a day spent smoking rather than doing something productive. People write books in that amount of time.

Another benefit of not smoking is having more money. With the money saved by not smoking for a month, I can buy needed clothes or make a monthly payment to buy a new computer. The money adds up, and it's like anything else: It happens a little bit at a time. Energy, money, and of course, the bottom line is health—three great benefits.

It's kind of nice thinking it might be different for my kids. My dad smoked, and both my grandfathers did too. For me, it was the manly thing to do. Everybody smoked on television and in the movies. And they don't do that much anymore. You hardly ever see somebody smoke on television or in a film now, and the kids get preventive instruction in school. My son came home the other day and lectured his mother, who still smokes, about what happens to your heart when you inhale. Everything in your heart constricts. He had the whole thing he'd learned in his health class down. The health class was about blood circulation, but they talked about smoking, and I'm sure that smoking facts will be part of every organ system they cover in school. A subtle message is there that isn't so subtle after all, and I don't think my kids will smoke.

I think a good way to stop smoking, if someone wants to try, is to make a promise to yourself to stop for the next hour and see how easy it is. You can do it an hour at a time that way. Just get a clean glass and stand by the sink if you have to. You find that you must fill that time. You're not going to be able to avoid having the urge that cries for a cigarette. So you sweep the kitchen floor or change the oil in the car. Just do something. But if it's possible to stop for an hour, then it's possible to stop for good. And everybody stops for an hour, unless they don't sleep. Everybody becomes a nonsmoker in his or her sleep.

Connie's Story

Connie, age thirty-six, is a human resources professional as well as a mountain climber and tournament squash player by avocation; she loves her new Victorian home, indulging in sauna time, and good books.

I began smoking when I was twelve or thirteen. Every day I walked to school with three girls who were a year older, and we'd stop in the park so they could have a cigarette on the way. It wasn't long until I wanted to be like them and have a cigarette too. My parents would have thought it was uncool, definitely. I'd leave in the morning about ten minutes before my sister, even though we'd both be going to the same school and walking the same route. It was a little perplexing to my family that I'd leave ten minutes before her, but to smoke with my friends, I had to leave early. None of us kids were allowed to smoke at home.

I didn't really become a regular smoker, smoking heavily, until we went on summer vacation while I was in high school. We were restricted at school, and many of my activities didn't allow me to smoke. But by the time I went to college, I had full freedom, and I was smoking a lot. However, "a lot" in those days wasn't as much for me then as it was later.

Interestingly enough, I had a few friends who were smoking then, but I always hung out with a physically active crowd, and many of them didn't smoke. That was a major hurdle. Philosophically, smoking presented me with a conflict. My first boyfriend in college was a downhill skier, and he hated smoking. He was so disgusted with it that I had to use mouthwash before he would kiss me. I was so stubborn about my smoking. However, the cognitive dissonance of it started to wear on me even back then because it really did not fit with what I valued. It was awkward for me to smoke because of the things I liked to do. For instance, it was awkward to smoke while riding a chair lift.

But I kept smoking, and sometime later I applied to be an instructor at the Minnesota Outward Bound School. The guy was coming out to interview me at my home, and I'd never met him before. I'd warned my roommate not to talk about smoking. I wanted to impress the rep from the school and show him that I could really do this job. We set up the house to make it look outdoorsy; my hiking boots were near the door. He said, "Let's go to a Chinese restaurant. I hear there's one nearby." I called upstairs to my roommate to see if she knew where the place was, and she called back down, "Oh yes, that's where you bought a pack of cigarettes the other day." I about died. That blew my cover, but I got the job anyway. This was during my junior year in college.

While I worked for Outward Bound that summer, I didn't smoke openly; but I would sneak around to smoke. I kept my smoking hidden for three months, and I thought I was getting away with it. of course, now I realize that when you're in the woods for thirty days, everyone knows what's going on, so they knew I was sneaking smokes, but I thought I was hiding it. Besides how everyone notices what you're doing in a setting like that, I'm sure they smelled it on me.

Many years later, I started going out with another man I didn't want to have seen me smoking. By this time, I was in such inner conflict over my habit that I decided I wasn't going to smoke in front of him. We went out a few times, and I didn't smoke. But I couldn't maintain it. One night when we went out together for dinner, I told him I smoked. He had known it all along. Nobody is ever really fooled.

I was well prepared for smoking from childhood on because I grew up in a smoking household. My parents both smoked, but they stopped. My mother says that for her, quitting was almost a religious experience. And my father stopped by using a "one day at a time" concept. He still says he just does not smoke for right now. He more or less used the A.A. "one day at a time" philosophy without knowing anything about A.A. My siblings and I all smoked, but I was the diehard smoker. I was the most obviously addicted one out of the whole family. I smoked the most, and I was the least open about it. Also, I was the first one to stop. My brother has now quit too, so we have two down and three to go. But I smoked for years before I quit, even though it interfered with my value system.

A few years after college, I went on an expedition to Mt. McKinley in Alaska. I didn't smoke cigarettes during my twelve weeks of training, but I smoked a pipe. Philosophically, it seemed acceptable to pull out the pipe. There I was, dying from the strain, skiing up to the base of Mt. McKinley–and yet still preoccupied with smoking. I never got off nicotine during that time. Even though I wasn't smoking any cigarettes, I still got my nicotine, and that was a true pleasure. It was one of life's small pleasures during that time, and just not smoking cigarettes was a big thing for me.

Smoking had such importance to me that it got in the way of a lot of my activities. I remember getting ready to go on a six-day mountain climb and carefully packing my cigarettes. I ignored the paradox. I remember many trips with Outward Bound–twelve-day backpacking trips–and carrying enough cigarettes to last throughout the trip. I would take along enough for me, and then if there was someone else on the trip who was starting to borrow cigarettes, I'd guard my stash. There was no way I could get any further supply where I was. I remember one trip when I'd misjudged my rations, or maybe I'd lost a couple of packs in the water or something. I rationed myself to three a day, only occasionally taking a hit off one. Then I would tap it out just to make sure I never was without.

I really didn't like my cigarette habit. I was very ashamed about my activities. Most people were really surprised that I smoked. I was self-conscious about it. Many people have told me I was a very respectful smoker. Because I really didn't want others to remember that I smoked, I was very conscious of where my smoke was going. For instance, if I was on a camping or backpacking trip, I would only smoke around the campfire in the evening when people wouldn't notice it so much. Almost from day one, I was hiding my habit, trying to be subtle about it. I attempted to be inconspicuous with my smoking; I was only open about it at a big party or something where a lot of people were smoking and vaping.

I first began thinking of quitting smoking while I was still in my late teens. Mom and Dad said that they would pay my siblings and I if we stopped smoking by the time we were twenty-one. But I didn't. The Mt. McKinley trip got me thinking about it, but I decided that going on the trip was enough to manage. Quitting crossed my mind a lot, but I didn't do much about it, although I started asking others who had stopped how they'd done it. I loved hearing other people's stories about how they had stopped. I was curious about it because I knew I wanted to quit someday. I talked about stopping smoking, but not about *me* stopping smoking. I picked up flyers and I read articles and ads about stop-smoking programs. I never went to any of them, but I always read up on the subject with interest, and I began to cut the articles out and save them.

Then my brother went to a hypnotist in New York to quit smoking. I was living in New York too, and he and I were together right after his visit to the hypnotist. He was so calm, and he simply stopped smoking. I was really impressed. I referred another friend of mine to a hypnotist, and he quit too. I thought, wow, this must really be something else. By this time, I'd moved away from New York, but I made an appointment with the hypnotist and flew back there, ostensibly to visit friends, but my real reason was to go to see the hypnotist. I didn't tell anybody what I was doing except the people I was visiting in Connecticut. I wanted a cigarette so bad.

But I did go to the hypnotist, and I kept the recording he made of what he'd said. However, I knew it didn't feel right when I left that Friday. His process was to ask me why I wanted to stop, what I didn't like about smoking, and what I was doing there. During the hypnosis session, he repeated back exactly what I'd told him: Smoking was a value conflict for me. I really liked the act of smoking, but because I valued my health and liked physical exercise, smoking got in my way. My lungs hurt a lot during some of my activities, and I was embarrassed that I smoked. It didn't fit with my inner self-image. But I stopped for only two days. I bought a little audio player so I could listen to the hypnosis recording that he'd given me, but it didn't help. The second I left my friends' house, I went straight to the train station and bought a pack of cigarettes. I kept that experience private as my little inward secret. But I don't chastise myself at all for that, and I don't chastise other people for their attempts to stop. I think that's all part of being ready. I made no other real attempts to quit.

I liked smoking; I liked the ritual of it. I associated smoking with slowing down, it felt calming and a little bit soothing. I liked the taste, except I didn't like what it meant. Still, sitting around and talking on the phone while having cigarettes and coffee was a pretty nice way to spend a couple of hours.

Even though I pretended for years that I smoked only a pack a day, I'm sure I was smoking at least two packs a day. And as I started thinking about stopping, I actually smoked more because I knew that I was going to be quitting. I always had a carton around.

When I really got serious about stopping, I talked to a lot of people to get ideas about how to do it. I remember one conversation that really hit me. I was with a friend in a restaurant. She said rather than feeling deprived after quitting, become a nonsmoker instead. That approach was similar to how my father had done it. It made more sense to me at that time than it had twenty years earlier when my dad did it.

There wasn't any event in my life to prepare me like a horrible cancer story. I had thought about quitting on D-Day; although I didn't dare say to anyone that I was planning to actually stop on D-Day, I did commit myself to not smoking on that day. A friend at work asked me if he could use me to advertise D-Day in an article for the company newsletter. His article implied that I might be thinking about quitting for a longer time than just one day, and I was really ticked off at him. I wasn't planning to do that.

Before D-Day, I decided I wanted to do everything to stack the cards to my advantage. So I dusted off my hypnosis recordings, and I bought another self-help hypnosis recording so that I had two available hypnosis options. And I got Nicorette nicotine gum. I remember being high, sort of excited, wound up, and full of high energy that first day. In fact, my quitting tobacco lasted longer than just D-Day. I made myself listen to that hypnosis session twice a day, come hell or high water. And I did not let other things get in the way. I'm usually not quite that disciplined, but I was very disciplined about listening to the stop-smoking recordings. Not smoking was my top priority, and I really pushed myself to keep it that way. I chewed the Nicorette gum, and I didn't apologize for doing it. I wrestled with doing the gum because I knew it was nicotine. I think a placebo might have worked just as well. I chewed two or three pieces a day for a couple months. I got mouth sores, and they were really awful. Then I weaned myself from the gum; I got down to chewing one piece a day. I set a deadline for myself, and I quit. I actually had two or three pieces of gum left, but I decided I didn't want to do it anymore.

After quitting, I gained weight. My appetite really increased. Someone had told me that grapefruit would clear the nicotine out of my system faster, so I ate a lot of grapefruit and drank grapefruit juice. I really believe it helped. I never before ate as much grapefruit as I did in those first few days. With as much fruit as I was eating, it's no wonder my mouth was sore.

After quitting, I exercised a little bit more as well. I did it almost as a substitute. I wanted to feel the positive effects of not smoking, so I increased my exercise program. Surprisingly, it didn't feel as good to me as I hoped, at least not as soon as I would have expected. In spite of having smoked for twenty-some years, I thought that one week after stopping, I'd feel much better out on the squash court, but it really didn't work that way. I was deeply fascinated with what might be happening with my body, so I started reading some articles. I wanted to learn how long it would take for my lungs to regenerate. It takes five to ten years to replace the tissue if you smoked as long as I did. I've got a ways to go before my body is totally cleared out, but it's well its way to being cleansed.

Emotionally speaking, it wasn't that difficult for me to stop. I was really ready. I didn't want to be a smoker anymore. And I developed a little theory that I call the 51 percent theory. Fifty-one percent of me wanted to be a nonsmoker. And as long as the ratio was 51 to 49, I wouldn't smoke. I still wanted to smoke, but I mentally pictured these two little bodies inside my stomach that would go to battle whenever I wanted a cigarette, and the 51 percent character always won. Whenever I wanted a cigarette, I just closed my eyes and said, "Now you two deal with it." It was important that more of me wanted to not smoke than to smoke. That made all the difference. I believe that when you're ready to quit, when the time is right, then it isn't that much of a struggle. I really wanted not to smoke anymore.

I love the freedom of not smoking. I feel so much freer, going places and being with people. Smoking really ruled me more than I'd like to admit. It really controlled what I would do and wouldn't do—like running, for instance. I knew I could never be a serious runner while smoking. I run now, although I'm still not a serious runner. But it isn't an absurdity to think I could actually *really* run. The same with other sports—I can really go ahead and do whatever activities I want now, and I don't have a struggle with smoking. When I joined the squash club, it used to be that I was the only one who would come out after a game and light up a cigarette.

Other things have changed as well. One day, a coworker asked if I'd like to carpool with him to a meeting. I knew I'd have to be in the car for an hour not smoking, so I said no. I was bothered by meetings and movies, times when you knew you were going to have a block of time when you couldn't smoke. I was always aware of that, and now I'm free. The freedom is the biggest benefit of not smoking. I feel much better physically even though I have gained weight. I decided early on I wasn't going to let the weight gain bother me too much because I think it will adjust itself over time. It hasn't been quite a year, and I've stabilized. I don't feel like I'm gaining anymore. I think I've hit the top of the pyramid, and now I'm on the downside.

It's wonderful not being in conflict with my values anymore. I think quitting is the best thing I've ever done for myself. Smoking had haunted me since the beginning of my teens. When I first stopped smoking, I was a little hesitant to talk much about it because I didn't trust I'd be able to follow through with it. But I had a couple key friends who knew I was doing it, and that was good, because I needed support. I couldn't talk with my parents about it much even though they'd stopped smoking, because I wasn't sure I could go through with it. Mostly I was quiet about it.

I have not become a self-righteous nonsmoker. I hated it when someone was self-righteous around me. I try to be empathetic toward smokers because I know that they probably don't like the fact that they're smoking. However, it does bother me a bit. I hate being in a car with all the windows closed with a smoker.

I've come to believe that if people want to quit, they should allow themselves to celebrate not smoking. They should see it as a choice, and as something they want to do for themselves. They should give themselves permission to eat a little more. They shouldn't beat up on themselves if they don't do it right the first time, but think of it as a step in the right direction.

One thing that helped me gain strength was that I literally looked at myself in the mirror more than once and said, "You are a nonsmoker, and you want to stay that way." I did a lot of self-talk; that and the 51 percent theory gave me strength. Relying on these two tools meant I didn't have to deal with the urge anymore. I turned it over to those two little inner voices, and I didn't have to struggle with wanting a cigarette for very long after that. Another thing I did was pamper myself. I took saunas, and I also put a couple dollars away every day in a straw basket to spend on something I really wanted. After a couple weeks of saving, I took those dollars, bought myself a world map, and had it mounted. To this day, that world map is very special because it's connected to the new me. I also treated myself to buying magazines like *Glamour* and *Vogue*. I usually never spent money on things like that.

I did worry at first about my productivity. I was an early riser who always smoked and drank coffee while doing good work really early in the morning before going to my job. And I can't do that anymore. That bothers me some, but it's not worth going back to smoking for it. There is nothing that I can think of that would be worth my starting again. I think I'm a lifer. I get a little worried saying that because it's only been a year, but I really don't want to smoke again. And I think I'm free.

Tim's Story

Tim, age thirty-four, is married, a computer buff who excels in management.
He loves photography and mind puzzlers and is well-read in current affairs,
interests that feed his love of good conversation.

Smoking brought me a sense of belonging. I decided when I was in high school that I would not smoke because it wasn't good for me. I remember getting lectured about smoking by a couple of older guys who used to lifeguard. Also, most of my friends didn't smoke. Since there was a group of us who didn't smoke, it was easier not to start.

I went to college for a year and didn't smoke. After that year, I dropped out of school because I had been given a high draft lottery number. I decided that I was going to seek my fame and fortune and set off on a little odyssey. I was going to go to Mexico, but Paul, a friend of mine, was living in Phoenix. I stopped by to see him and ended up staying. I hung out with him and his friends, and they smoked. We used to sit in a pancake restaurant, and we'd pool our money for an endless pot of coffee. We'd drink coffee all night with lots of cream and sugar and smoke cigarettes. We had a 'leader' of our little group who was quite a bit older than the rest of us, and he set the tone. We drank our coffee the way he liked it. I really started smoking because of peer pressure. They weren't trying to get me to smoke, but I wanted to be like them, so I smoked. It seemed really cool.

I had experimented a little bit with smoking when I was much younger. I remember once picking some weeds that were called Indian tobacco. I tried smoking that plant and scorched my lungs. For a couple of days in the ninth grade, I briefly hung out with some guys who smoked, and I remember stealing some cigarettes from my grandmother and smoking them. I got sick trying to be cool, and I couldn't imagine ever smoking for real.

Smoking for real in Phoenix wasn't easy at first. Even drinking the coffee was hard. I had to put lots of cream and sugar in it to dilute it; and then I really had to work at smoking cigarettes. As I recall, my friends mildly discouraged me from smoking because it was so hard for me. Our brand was Benson & Hedges, the "sophisticated" brand at the time, which was kind of a joke because we were consciously trying not to be sophisticated. It probably took me a good month or so before I could really smoke a pack a day. But then I got addicted.

Smoking brought me a sense of belonging, and very soon, of course, smoking became a good old friend. When I'd light one up, I'd feel better. It was both social and ceremonial. We had these really intense discussions about human needs while drinking coffee and puffing up a storm at the pancake house. I had good associations with smoking at that time.

After smoking for about a year, I felt like I should quit. I was living in Chicago at the time. One day I was playing Frisbee in a parking lot, and I was so winded I couldn't believe it. It was such a foreign experience to feel so out of breath. I figured I needed to quit smoking. One day shortly thereafter, I did throw away my pack—until I retrieved it about five in the afternoon. I tried to quit a couple times while living in Chicago, but it never went anywhere. I stopped smoking Benson & Hedges and switched to Old Golds before moving back home and returning to school.

I was living with friends, and I remember vividly when Tom, Bob, and I decided we were going to quit smoking. We were all going to the university. At the time, I had a part-time job as a Xerox machine operator. One Sunday night, we swore off cigarettes, and on Monday, we all went off to class with no cigarettes. I made it a whole week, but it was really hard. On Friday night, we were going to a party after I got off work. I went into my boss's office to punch my time card, and there was a pack of cigarettes on her desk. Nobody would know if I had one. I looked around; I took a cigarette out and held it, rolling it in my hands, and then I said, "Nope! I quit. I'm not having it." I was so proud of myself. I went to the party, and Tom and Bob were smoking. Bob had snuck a cigarette on Tuesday, and I felt so betrayed. I lit up a cigarette, and I was back smoking a pack a day within a day or two.

I didn't think smoking was a good thing to be doing, but I didn't think it was all that bad a thing to be doing either. I knew that there were health risks associated with it, but I minimized them or joked about it. Several of the people I hung out with smoked, so it was really a social thing.

About a year after that, I met Mary, who is now my wife. When she started treatment for chemical dependency, I felt like I should quit something too; so I quit cigarettes. It was sort of a noble cause. That was the only reason I was trying to quit. I would not have been motivated to try and quit otherwise. It was physically difficult to quit; psychologically and emotionally, I was very upset because her counselor wouldn't let me see or talk to her. After Mary had been in treatment for a couple weeks, I went with my friend, Marty, and his girlfriend from Chicago to the Boundary Waters of Minnesota. I was still in withdrawal from the nicotine, and I was emotionally messed up about Mary being in treatment. I didn't know what was happening. I really missed the cigarettes because I had used them to kill emotional pain, and I had a lot of that kind of pain in those years.

Stop Smoking and Vaping Now!

I remember telling myself that I couldn't really quit if I'm quitting for someone else or with someone else. Thinking back to when I'd quit with Bob and Tom, I really wasn't motivated. I felt more like I was quitting for me when Mary was in treatment, and I stayed off cigarettes for a couple of years that time, even though Mary still smoked.

At times, though, it was difficult being around a smoker. Some of the worst times were at parties. If I had anything to drink, I instantly wanted a cigarette. I remember a guy telling me there was actually some kind of chemical association between the two. It felt like that for me, but I didn't give in. I felt that if Mary could manage to not drink, then I could handle not smoking.

I started smoking again almost three years later. I had broken up with Mary that fall, and we'd gone our separate ways. I had finished college and gotten through a quarter of graduate school before I dropped out. I was majorly involved with some other men in meditation training. I was working and doing meditation. These friends smoked quite heavily, although I had not restarted yet. We did a training that was twelve weeks long that first spring. It was pretty intense, and I did a couple of other meditation programs that winter. Throughout training, there was no smoking and no caffeine allowed during the week, although we could drink caffeine on the weekends. We had a particular diet to follow, too, except nobody did. These guys had to quit smoking. It was an intense experience, and we had a little closing ceremony at the end of the twelve weeks. There was a sense of accomplishment because we had abstained from a variety of things. Finishing the training was worth celebrating. The guys were thrilled because they could have a cigarette, although nobody smoked that first night. Then, the next day, we all smoked, even me. I really got into it again, and for quite a while I smoked.

I quit again for a brief time when I got sick. I did that several times. Whenever I was sick, I didn't want to smoke. I'd go three, four, or five days without smoking but then start again. The next major time I quit was with Mary. We had gotten back together and married. We both joined a health club in order to clean up our act. We quit smoking and began to work out. It was really hard, even painful. Both physically and psychologically, the withdrawal was really intense. I had an incredible craving for nicotine. It was like a third hand reaching out of my chest for a cigarette. I got through the cravings using intense overexercise. I started swimming and chewed a lot of gum and used sheer force of will. The exercise was definitely helpful. I also ate more sugar.

After being off cigarettes for three or four months, we went on a trip. Mary hadn't lasted as long as I had; after about two months, she had started smoking again, which made it very hard for me. I really felt betrayed, and it was annoying to be around her when she was smoking.

It still wasn't easy for me not to smoke, but I was doing okay. We went on our trip in this little bitty car with Mary puffing away. It was an extremely stressful situation. We'd been to my stepbrother's wedding, and we were heading east. We drove for an hour and a half before realizing we'd forgotten the music mix we'd made for the trip, so then we drove back to get it. We lost three hours, and we ran into an incredible rainstorm. Before long, my adrenaline was pumping and I was totally stressed out. Mary was smoking, and finally, when the weather broke a little, I lit a cigarette. So we had smoking in common again. It was like a social lubricant. At a very physical level, smoking with a friend was establishing a meaningful connection, a real bond. By this time, Mary and I were having lots of difficulties in our relationship, and smoking was one of the few things that we could share.

I really got rolling on smoking again on that trip. I continued smoking heavily from that fall until the next spring. I kept saying I should quit, but I didn't, not until I got a call from my mom one night. I was home alone, sitting at my desk smoking cigarettes. She told me that my dad was in the hospital, and he had cancer. The surgery was already scheduled. I took the cigarette out of my mouth and put it out. That was my last cigarette. Smoking was not fun anymore. I really had a different motivation this time. I knew smoking was dangerous. It really hit home that smoking could kill me. I was through kidding myself.

The next two days were just awful, but then it was pretty much over. In many respects, it was the easiest time I ever had quitting. The first morning, my nerve endings were just screaming from the withdrawal; because of my dad's illness, I was not in a good place anyway. I was freaked out. I'd always used cigarettes to suppress my emotions, and facing what was happening with my dad with no emotional painkiller was horrible. It was just too awful to feel. Everything was too loud, and too close. I lived through two days of hell. And then it seemed to pass. For that I was immensely grateful. My Higher Power was able to make it easier for me. I couldn't handle much of anything at the time.

It's about three and a half years now since I've smoked. I've learned that trying to quit for someone else is a lot harder. Having a more vivid sense of the health risks due to my dad's health situation gave me motivation that I didn't have the other times I quit.

The benefits of not smoking are great. I'm no longer destroying my clothes and my furniture on a regular basis. My wife and I had spent a few thousand dollars on a really nice sofa that has been irreparably damaged by our smoking. I no longer burn my fingers on a regular basis while drawing the cigarette out of my mouth. I'm not an especially uncoordinated person, but I used to pull the core out between my index and middle fingers and burn myself. I feel a lot better physically. I'm exercising regularly, and I'm in much better shape than I ever believed possible. Even at times when I don't exercise at all, I'm still in much better shape. I no longer have chronic colds all winter long. I think I probably did permanent inner damage to my nose by smoking, although I don't have sinus problems anymore. One of the benefits of quitting is that even if you have damaged all those nerves and membranes in your nose, you still can taste things a lot

Stop Smoking and Vaping Now!

better. I like the way things smell. Our house and my new car smell so good, and there are no burns in this car's upholstery.

I'm pretty confident I'll never smoke again, although I don't think I would bet my life on it. If the people really close to me started again, it would make it harder for me. But I have a realization that I hadn't really fully integrated before at a gut level about how harmful smoking is.

I'm a happy nonsmoker. I like not smoking, and I don't miss it; when I see other people smoking, I'm glad it's not me. I'm free, I hope forever.

Marjorie's Story

Marjorie, age fifty-seven, is a divorced mother of four who is also a recovering alcoholic.
She loves people, plants, and horses and is active in community affairs.

The first time I smoked was when I was fifteen. I was with a friend whom I rode horses with; in fact, we were working with our horses that first time I smoked. A lot of people I knew smoked. My mother smoked, and all of my friends were beginning to smoke too. I smoked for most of my high school years until I was a senior. At that time, I wanted a new horse; there was one in particular I wanted very badly, so I made a deal with my father. If he'd buy me the horse, I wouldn't smoke until I was twenty-one, and I would get on the "A" honor roll. I would have sold my soul for that particular animal. I quit without any difficulty and didn't start again for a while, although I did restart smoking before reaching age twenty-one.

I started again in college during my freshman year. Most of my friends smoked. I preferred to smoke. It was like a good companion. I was not very socially adept; when out on a date or at a party, smoking gave me something to do, particularly if I was at a loss for words. For nearly forty years I smoked.

When I hit my forties, I began to notice I was becoming short of breath, and I knew it was from the smoking. I was leading an extremely active outdoor life by then, and whenever I had to run, I was in trouble. My husband and I had bought a farm, and I ended up with a horse boarding stable where I kept my own horses plus taking in boarders. I ended up giving riding lessons. I hadn't intended for my business to get that big. The horse business is like that. It was a busy time for me. I was working in the barn and riding every day, and I was on my feet teaching lessons. Aside from my smoking and drinking, I was physically very fit. The shortness of breath from smoking was not bad enough to consider quitting. Besides, I had a lot of denial. Other people would get emphysema (COPD) and lung cancer, but I wouldn't.

In these last ten or twelve years of my life, many things have changed that I hadn't counted on. For one, I quit drinking. I got divorced. I changed my vocation; I trained as a chemical dependency counselor and worked at that for a while. But I decided that wasn't what I wanted to do. Through all of this, I had a lot of emotional pain, and I kept on smoking. In A.A., there was always support for smoking. Only very recently has there been enough awareness to create favor for nonsmoking A.A. groups.

I began to realize in the last five years that my physical stamina wasn't what I wanted it to be. It was clear it was deteriorating. Going up and down stairs in my two-story house was getting harder all the time. I was averaging about a pack and a half a day, and I had been doing it for a long time. One of the reasons that I had never tried to stop, even when I was experiencing health consequences, was because I was positive I couldn't do it, and that potential failure was not something I wanted to see made real. I felt doomed to keep on smoking. I was not taking part in physical activities because I knew it would be too hard for me. About six years ago, I tried to play racquetball with a friend; I almost died. I decided not to do *that* again, and that's why I don't play tennis anymore. At the present time, I'm trying to force myself to take walks, but I've never liked walking. I always thought walking was an extraordinarily boring way to spend time. So much has changed since I no longer have the horses. I'm not living that terribly active outdoor life anymore. Everything about my physical life and circumstances has changed.

Before I stopped, many of my friends began talking to me about quitting smoking. I was very cool about it, but I felt terribly defensive inside. I realized my breathing sounded bad, and that was embarrassing. That was another reason I would not exert myself in certain ways when I was around people. I didn't want them to notice. Eventually I realized that unless I did something about my smoking, I was going to need one of those cute little portable respirators for sure. I just knew it. I wasn't afraid of cancer. Somehow or other cancer was not a concern of mine. I wasn't afraid of dying of lung cancer, but I was afraid of living with a little oxygen tube in my nose. They don't look very cute.

I kept putting off quitting, but I was beginning to say to myself, every time I lit a cigarette, this is it. This new internal dialogue was beginning to take place, but it took two years of self-talk for me to quit. I sort of tiptoed around it, looking over my shoulder every now and then. I'd look, but I wasn't able to face the issue squarely.

Finally, I tried a couple of things to help me quit. On a whim one day, I bought antismoking stuff that you chew at the drugstore. It was not Nicorette gum. These were tablets that made your cigarettes taste absolutely awful. I brought the tablets home, stuck them in the back of my closet, and left them there. Six months or a year later, I dug them out, thinking, oh, gee, maybe I'll try this. At first I was able to cut down on my smoking; but just like with controlling my drinking, after a while, it was too hard. Early on, though, I was very encouraged by my ability to cut down some, and thought, well, at least I know that I can manage to smoke less. It was a very slow process for me. But I found that I couldn't keep it up. It was just too hard. And so I let the whole thing go for a while and returned to smoking just like before.

Next, I talked with someone about acupuncture. It was probably six months after that when I actually got acupuncture. At the same time, I also got a Nicorette gum prescription from my doctor. I also got some information about a Twelve Step program for quitting smoking. Participating in the Twelve Step program didn't work at all for me. Although I'd never liked gum, chewing the Nicorettes was somewhat helpful during my physical withdrawal from nicotine. The acupuncture also helped at first, but the effect wasn't long-lasting. I think all the acupuncture did was mask the withdrawal symptoms. However, by using all of these tools, I managed not to smoke for about a week, which was an improvement. But again it was just too hard not to smoke. It was just too hard. So I ended up going back to it. I started by thinking, oh, I'll just have one. I can't remember how long it took me to get back up to my daily pack and a half, but it was not long enough.

A short time later, I was at a meeting, and a woman about my age announced that she hadn't smoked for a full year. I didn't know her very well, but I sort of pricked up my ears. I wanted to know what she had done—what worked for her. So I asked her about it. She had gone through a program called Clean Break. She had previously tried acupuncture and many other things without success. Clean Break was what at last worked for her. Shortly after hearing her story, I saw an ad for Clean Break. The ad said if you're interested in quitting, just bring your cigarettes and an open mind. That's what I did. In many ways, it's a hardline program; and in some ways, it's like A.A. because it's taught by ex-smokers—not doctors. The guy who ran the session I went to said, "You're all a bunch of junkies." You could just feel the tension in the room.

They talked a lot about deprivation. Deprivation is what makes people return to smoking. They gave us some tools to help us deal with that. One of the tools was telephone counseling. We could call a group leader anytime for support, and the leader called me twice a week. He said that one of the reasons people fail when they try to stop smoking is they immediately want to call themselves nonsmokers. He didn't believe it was possible for a smoker to ever really feel like a nonsmoker. He said, "It's a little bit like turning back into a cucumber after you're pickled." Not everyone will agree with all parts of this program, but it helped me. However, I've never been so sick in my life as since I stopped smoking.

It has been about a year and a half since I smoked, and I've never felt so bereft in my life. Smoking was like my lover, and giving it up made me feel abandoned. The reason I quit when I did was because I was planning a trip to Canada. I knew I would be hiking a lot, and I wanted not to be so short of breath. I felt fine on the trip; I walked all over the place, and I wasn't breathless. I had also planned a trip to England after the Canadian trip. But when I landed at the airport, I couldn't breathe. I could barely make it from the airplane through the airport to the bus that was going to take us to where my friend and I were going. Although the doctors in England couldn't find anything wrong with me, I could barely get out of bed. I ended up coming home early. I felt like I was living in a dead body. I was scared. I was literally only able to do the bare minimum necessary for survival. I went to my doctor back home, and he couldn't find a thing wrong with me either. That was even more disturbing.

Finally a friend took me to a chiropractor and holistic healer. She gave me adrenaline and diagnosed a number of problems in ways that made perfect sense to me. She said that my entire system had become so dependent on the stimulation provided by nicotine that it had just quit working without it.

I'm still in the process of getting back to normal. I'm doing very little. I had started a business with a friend, but I had to drop out. I just couldn't keep it up. Emotionally, I was a mess. I've come to the conclusion that I used cigarettes to cope in such an extensive way that it was like losing the Band-Aid. I had no idea how important nicotine was in my life. Without it, I cried inappropriately. The only reason I haven't gone back to smoking is that I want to live more than I want to die. And I never want to go through quitting again. I'd rather sober up every other week from alcohol than ever again go through what I have in the past year and a half. This has been the hardest effort I've ever put in—ever! I couldn't have made it without friends I could just babble to; and babble I did. It did not occur to me to go to a Smokers Anonymous group. I didn't have the energy.

Although not smoking has been very hard, there are some pluses; the best thing about not smoking is being free of the control it had over me. I like not having to run back and get my cigarettes or make sure I have them whenever I go out. I'm not yet feeling all that much better physically than before I stopped, but I am breathing a little better. I've put on more weight than I wanted to, but I was terribly underweight when I quit smoking, so that's probably not all bad.

Also, I'm no longer fighting with myself all the time now that I've quit. I had reached the point where I was feeling guilty every time I lit a cigarette, and that was not fun. I'm free now of the preoccupation with cigarettes. But I think the most important thing someone needs in order to successfully quit is a good support group. Although it took me several attempts to quit smoking, I'm glad I kept trying.

Recently I've realized that how I think about myself has changed a lot since I quit. The change is the result of not smoking, but it's not only the not smoking. I'm more concerned these days with getting physically healed and getting some energy back. I've gotten into more psychological and emotional growth as well. For me, stopping smoking has triggered a whole new phase of living. My feelings are no longer muffled. Smoking was how I coped with emotional things and with issues of all kinds. The Band-Aid has been removed, but the owie is still there. Sometimes it's threatening. Sometimes it's infuriating, because growth is terribly, terribly slow. There are times when I would much prefer to be back where I was as a smoker, but it would be really stupid to start smoking again, and I don't like thinking of myself as stupid.

I remember going to work right after I quit and being absolutely good for nothing at all. I literally did not know what I was doing or where I was going. I had to be led around by my hand, which in a sense can be very reinforcing. I did find out that my friends loved me no less when I was a blithering idiot. That was strengthening. I think smoking is an addiction for so many of us. There aren't many people like my mother, who managed to quit by tapering off. It's for certain that I couldn't do it like that.

Quitting is the hardest thing I've ever done; I have no explanation for it. I used smoking as a substitute for everything, and a year and a half since leaving it behind, I'm still in the process of grieving. It's almost as if the deprivation of cigarettes was like a magnet, and everything in my life that I'd never grieved was drawn to the surface. This has been a very difficult period for me. I find I need a lot of reassurance in the concept that this too shall pass. But I'm hopeful. And I'm glad I'm no longer smoking. I've learned it is possible to live without smoking, and I was not sure of that a little more than eighteen months ago.

Stop Smoking and Vaping Now!

"I HAD TO QUIT LYING TO MYSELF ABOUT CIGARETTES"

John's Story

John, age twenty-eight, is an engineer. Married and a new father, he is a talented trumpet player, a woodworking hobbyist, and a home remodeler.

I started smoking on a work crew with a bunch of kids my age. We were digging trenches for phone lines. I was about fifteen, and I wanted to feel as though I belonged. One of the group had a pack of cigarettes so we all smoked. Up to that point, the kids I hung out with didn't smoke. Peer pressure had a lot to do with my starting.

I remember the very first time; it was powerful stuff. It made me dizzy, and my heart pounded. The rush of the drug really got me. It wasn't really pleasurable. Actually, I felt nauseous, but in order to maintain my "in" with the group, I kept doing it. And then the queasy effects became less intense. From age fifteen on, I was a regular smoker, and I smoked a pack a day.

While growing up, before I started smoking, I more or less expected to smoke eventually (because many of my older brothers did) even though I was into athletics a bit. Many of my older sisters smoked too. My mother never smoked, and my father only smoked a pipe for a while when I was very, very young. I don't think he ever smoked cigarettes.

By the time I was sixteen, I had reduced my athletics to just skiing. I was on the ski team, but I didn't compete, I just went out to ski. There were rules about not smoking, so I would hide out when I was doing it. I also played in the school band, and it was not considered acceptable to smoke in the band, but we hid it. Because my mother had fallen on her head years before, she had lost her sense of smell; thus, I was able to smoke at home and get away with it. She didn't approve of my smoking, but she couldn't tell when I was doing it.

In fact, my friends and I smoked pot as well as cigarettes in the basement. It was okay with my father if our friends smoked cigarettes in the house. That was acceptable. We couldn't, but it was okay if they did. If someone lit up a cigarette, then it didn't matter whether it was pot smoke or something else in the air. My friends smoking became a means of covering up the whole pot smoking situation.

I really enjoyed smoking from the very first, but it eventually became such an obsession. Early on, smoking ran me rather than my running it, though I did quit on more than one occasion for brief spells.

I was nineteen and a college student the first time I quit. I realized every time a tense situation came up, I reached for the cigarettes. The lie about smoking was that it was going to get me through the situation and I'd feel better. Smoking was going to handle the situation for me. That was the big lie, although I definitely believed it at the time.

I was a musician while in school. I played the trumpet in the band, and smoking affected my wind. It had become such an obsession by that time. I had already quit drinking, and suddenly I had an increased awareness about what was going on with my body. I was playing my horn a lot, and smoking was affecting my lung power, so I decided to quit. In preparation, I worked with a guy who did hypnosis with me. He was a university psychologist who worked in human development. He taught me self-hypnosis using visualization and meditation, as well as relaxation techniques to combine with the self-hypnosis. I saw him on a weekly basis for a couple of months while I was tapering down on my smoking. Eventually, I had some luck with staying off nicotine.

The hypnosis sessions were structured in three parts. We did visualization and meditation. For the meditation, I'd sit down, close my eyes, and take a deep breath to relax. Then I'd concentrate on three main principles. One was that smoking was poison for my body. The second one was about how I needed my body to live. The third principle was that I owed myself the respect of protection and consideration. He also instructed me to make some associations with pleasurable things that I would get out of not smoking. For instance, one was having better lung power to blow my horn so I could be really hot on my instrument; another was the ability to enjoy the taste of food again; then there was just getting rid of the messy habit of smoking. He helped me to remember enjoyable experiences from my past when I was a nonsmoker. He'd suggest that I visualize myself in a favorite place in the world; and then he'd bring me back to the three principles and thereby form an association between the two. This technique worked for me. Shortly thereafter, I was able to transfer to another university as a nonsmoker.

Unfortunately, that didn't last; by springtime, I was smoking again. The day I took it up again was a rough day. My car had failed to start, and I had to hitchhike to school. Who should come along but some of my old friends from high school whom I hadn't seen in quite some time. They picked me up and they were all smoking. At that point, I had not been keeping up with carrying out the daily three-point visualization and meditation program the hypnotist had taught me—and I started smoking again. It was just like the first time I ever smoked; I got the good rush. But this time I didn't experience nausea and dizziness with a pounding heart. None of the negative consequences were there. It felt good to smoke. After all, I was having a tough day, and I thought, why not? Smoking felt friendly and familiar.

I smoked for another four years then, but it wasn't long before it was not very satisfying. Once again, I had the delusion that it somehow made life's problems easier to handle. By the time I got around to working on quitting again, I was out of school and working as an engineer, trying to establish myself as a professional. Oftentimes people would call with difficult situations, and I'd find myself reaching for the pack of cigarettes. Again, I was haunted by the same lie—the belief that smoking would somehow help get me through those difficult situations. For me, one of the keys of successfully quitting was that I had to quit lying to myself about what cigarettes did and did not do for me.

Eventually, I reached a point of being fed up with the habit and how it had a hold on me. I wasn't in control of it. I realized that was a lie. Smoking never did help me through any situation. Talking with other people who were also struggling to quit was really helpful. On my twenty-fourth birthday, I quit for the last time, and that was four years ago on November 20.

I didn't choose to quit on my birthday for any special reason. I'd been hoping to quit for a long time, but still I was walking around with cigarettes. On that day, I'd left them in the car and was traveling from one place to another in my friend's vehicle—without my cigarettes. That was the first night I went without. It was tough. I had strong cravings, but as long as I kept myself occupied it was a little easier. The desire to smoke was mostly mental, but I think the mental craving is triggered by the physical reaction. I had been consistently smoking a pack a day, day after day.

After quitting, I began to involve myself with social groups where they didn't smoke. I sought out people who were either not smoking or who were also struggling not to smoke. I soon learned that no urge ever lasts more than thirty seconds. I could deal with each little urge and get through that half minute. I recalled that the first thing that happens when you take a drag off a cigarette is that you get a big breath of air as well; so I started just taking deep breaths. There's something that's just relaxing and satisfying about taking a big breath now. I was gentle with myself the day I finally quit. Finally quitting was the culmination of quite a period of working up to it.

Another tool that I learned about when I'd quit on an earlier occasion was when I found myself reaching for a cigarette, I'd draw my hand back and gently rub my cheek. I was changing my behavior and being nice to myself. You use the same movement to bring a cigarette up to your lips as to bring your hand up to your cheek, but a gentle touch on the cheek is like giving yourself a gift.

Even though I haven't smoked now for four years, there have been a couple times when I really wanted one—this would happen while I was getting together with other people who were enjoying their cigarettes. But generally, they look bad. They smell bad. I don't like to be around anyone who's smoking. I don't like them to be around me. I don't like for people to smoke in my house or car. When people unconsciously bring cigarettes over to where I am, I ask them not to smoke near me. More and more, the people I associate with don't smoke. I think that people who have quit are moving toward higher spiritual things and working on cleaning up their act in their entire life.

I had only smoked for eight years, which isn't long, but it did affect my lung capacity. It affected me a great deal. I thought smoking made me attractive, but that's hardly true. It turned people away from me that I might otherwise have met. I shun smokers now. I don't like to be around them because it offends me, so I'm sure others stayed away from me. I probably missed meeting some marvelous people.

There are so many rewards for not smoking, but the best reward is I'm no longer polluting the air. Also, my baby will grow up with a role model who doesn't smoke. That's important to me. I'm finding healthier ways to relax and more positive ways to deal with the trials of life. I relax through deep breathing, along with meditation and visualization. It really helps; it really calms me down. Not smoking is a conscious choice. Smoking was not a conscious choice. It was beyond choosing—it was habitual and automatic.

Whenever I feel I'm wavering, I remember the three-point meditation: Smoking is poison for my body. I need my body to live. I owe myself that respect. And then I visualize being able to taste my food, breathing deeply, and smelling good. The urges won't last more than thirty seconds. I don't beat myself up if I experience an obsessive longing for a cigarette. Any addiction is powerful stuff. My first cigarette just about knocked me over. In my mind, it's as hard as any other drug to give up, and it doesn't get you through tough situations. It doesn't make anything any easier. Smoking isn't handsome or beautiful or sophisticated. It's a lie to believe otherwise.

It's pretty rare now that I get an urge to smoke again, and I'm very happy not smoking. I'm really happy living in a house that doesn't smell like smoke. It feels safe knowing that we won't cause a fire due to careless smoking. It's nice to be alive. I get good feelings knowing that I'm free, that smoking isn't controlling me. My father died of cancer, not from smoking, but still it had a profound effect on me because smoking is so associated with cancer. I watched the slow disintegration of a very big man to a very small person. The cancer just ate him up. I feel good being alive, and I don't want to contribute in any way to an early and untimely death! Not smoking is a good choice for me.

Terence's Story

An attorney as well as a married father of four, Terence, age fifty, loves escaping to his getaway condo in Snowmass, Colorado, to ski.

I don't remember the first cigarette that I ever had, although I'm pretty sure I was about fifteen, and I smoked because everybody else was having a cigarette. Nobody in my family smoked, but all my friends did. We smoked Lucky Strikes or Chesterfields, and I became an avid smoker from the very start. It was a big thing to have a whole carton of smokes. Even though I started smoking with my friends, I smoked at home right away. Nobody objected. When I think back about it, I didn't particularly enjoy friends. I only smoked because everybody else did. It never did anything special for me, but I smoked anyway.

In most of the places I went, smoking was prohibited—at school, for example. But we smoked anyway and got caught on occasion. We'd have a cigarette before we went in to school. Generally we'd go somewhere out on the football field to smoke, far away from detection.

While in high school, I had a job at a drugstore. I very soon noted the only way I could get a break was to have a cigarette and a cup of coffee. I think I started smoking cigarettes and drinking coffee at the same time so that I could take a break. It was the one sure way to get one. I continued smoking when I went off to college. During this early period of my life, I never considered not smoking. I smoked all through college and law school. I smoked consistently until I was about thirty. Smoking had begun to feel like a good friend. Even now I can practically feel the cigarette between my fingers. If I take a deep breath, I get some satisfaction from the experience.

While I was in high school, most of my friends smoked, but in college very few did. In law school, there were even fewer people my age who smoked. Because of that, I experimented with stopping many times. I was not able to stop smoking for good the first time I tried.

As I recall, my first experience with trying to quit was prior to starting law school. I thought it would be good discipline for me not to smoke in law school. I'd be much smarter and much better in school, I thought. There must have been something detrimental about smoking in my mind, although I don't recall the specifics any longer. But after a very short time, I started smoking again. I wasn't able to go more than a day or two without a cigarette. I do remember though that even for just that day or two, I felt better.

The next time I remember quitting was four or more years later, after I had finished law school and married and was living in Washington. The surgeon general's report about the dangers of smoking was all over the media at that time. My wife quit smoking then, and she pressured me to quit. Once again, I did stop for a brief period, this time for a week or so. Soon thereafter, I started smoking again, but not at home. I smoked outside of the house on the sly. My wife could probably smell it on me. So she probably knew long before I admitted it to her that I was smoking. By this time, smoking was not consistent with my values, but I did it anyway.

I kept starting and stopping in those days, at least two or three more times. One time I had stopped; I was in New York, and it was very cold. I was very miserable, so I started smoking again. Another time I remember starting again was during a long automobile trip. I was moving back to my home state from Washington. I passed a drugstore advertising cartons of cigarettes for an incredibly reasonable price, so I got a carton for the trip home. I was traveling alone, and I proceeded to smoke all the way home. My wife had gone by plane. I was disappointed and felt guilty that I'd started again. By this time I figured that I wasn't able to quit. I felt that smoking was one of the few things that I wasn't able to control at that point in my life. I think that's why I kept trying to stop. But finally I was successful.

I was very sick at the time. I had the flu and could barely lift my head off the pillow, yet I was still looking for a cigarette. But it tasted awful, and it just made me feel more sick. I finally concluded that if it tasted that bad and if I could be that sick and still crave one, it was time to quit. Quitting was a little easier this time because I was so sick the first few days that I was off nicotine. At this point I had been smoking for twenty years.

For the first few years after quitting, my concentration wasn't good. My job requires heavy concentration, and part of my concentration ritual was to have a cigarette. Without the nicotine, I searched through a lot of potential substitutes. For a while, I used a pencil routine. I held the pencil between my fingers like a cigarette. It took a month or two before the really intense desire to smoke died down. It was another six months or more until the smell of a cigarette didn't make me want one. Often, if I had a drink, I'd want a cigarette. Since my pattern had been to have a cigarette after dinner, I began to eat chocolate sundaes as a substitute. Unlike some people, I didn't get into physical activity. I'm a skier now, but it wasn't something I took up to replace smoking. I didn't necessary get into healthier things as a result of not smoking. I considered not smoking enough all by itself.

I don't miss smoking anymore, but it took quite a while to get to that point. I did have a cigarette once in the early seventies. It was a victory celebration after an election, and everybody was having one. It tasted very good, but my wife and my friends quickly got on my case about it. I think if I'd had a second one, I would be smoking today. It's possible to go back, and I don't want to. I would all too quickly be right back to where I was before in no time, smoking a pack a day.

The best reward of not smoking is that I don't feel tied to cigarettes. I became dependent on them very quickly, and they became a part of everything that I did. While I was smoking, I couldn't enjoy things without having a cigarette.

One of the most difficult things about not smoking was that so many parts of my life had been invaded by cigarettes. Now, though, I feel good about having the genuine freedom to enjoy things without cigarettes.

My experience taught me that if you really want to quit, just keep trying. Even though I was not successful the first or the second or the third time, each time I tried, I learned a little more about myself and about what it took to quit. At some point, the right circumstances will come along and make it possible to stick with quitting. Getting support from others helps; although at the time that I quit, I didn't understand the value of support. My idea was that quitting was a matter of character. If I decided on a course of action, then I had to follow through no matter what. I was supposed to overcome whatever my problem was. That I failed to stay with quitting really bothered me.

Not as many people smoked by the time I quit, so I didn't have friends who could offer the kind of support that comes from shared experience. If I were quitting today, I'd sign up for a stop-smoking program and get that support, which would make it easier. But I'm glad that my personal experience of quitting is now behind me.

James's Story

James, age seventy-five, is a retired real estate developer and tax accountant. Married for decades with eight grown children, he enjoys gardening and participating in civic affairs.

I started smoking when I was about fifteen. My brother Leo, who was two years older, had already started. Originally, we always smoked together. Unfortunately, he was never able to quit even when he really needed to. He died of lung cancer when he was forty-six. He had willpower, strength, and character, but he could not quit smoking, even though he tried a thousand times. Leo and I used to have bets on quitting smoking at Lent. I could always quit for Lent, but he couldn't. I smoked from age fifteen on for better than fifty years, but I quit a bunch of times during that half century.

Growing up, most of the boys I knew smoked, with the exception of a couple of my older brothers. Smoking had only become popular in our community about ten years earlier. The thing I liked about smoking from the very first was the sedative feeling it gave me. It calmed me down a little bit. Another thing I liked was being like everyone else. It was the thing to do. While in high school, we always smoked in the john at recess. I imagine 75 percent of the boys smoked. Just twenty years earlier, almost nobody smoked.

One of the reasons it quickly became popular was that at the time, it was cheap. There were Lucky Strikes, Chesterfields, and Camels. There was one kind in a purple or light blue package, but I can't remember the brand. They were all small cigarettes; there were no filters and no king-size cigarettes back then. I think there was a little more tobacco in them back then and fewer chemicals, but they were still just as habit-forming. They were very, very tough to quit.

I started trying to quit smoking when I was only twenty. I was working my first real job, and I took a few bucks out of my first paycheck and sent away for a "how to quit smoking kit" that I saw advertised in a magazine. The program did not work for me. I wanted to quit because I didn't like to be controlled by cigarettes. I was not in control, and I wanted to quit permanently, but I just couldn't. I was however able to quit for Lent during twenty or thirty years, so I knew I could do it, but I'd always go back. One time I quit for a whole year. Back then, I used to frequently go on the wagon. I had been a drinker all my life, and when I'd periodically quit drinking, I'd notice that my need for cigarettes was greater. When I was drinking my usual amount, it was much simpler not to smoke much.

In time, I came to really understand that smoking was a terrible habit and a serious health hazard. When I finally had my lung operation, I was about sixty-eight. Nobody told me I had to quit when I'd had the operation, but I did, even though I didn't end up having lung cancer. I had two spots on my lungs that weren't cancer. Surprisingly, I didn't have any negative side effects from my smoking or my drinking for many years. Apparently, I had an unusual cast-iron stomach and constitution. However, the operation on my lungs proved to have terrible effects on me, even though the spots were benign. They had to break my ribs and everything. It took me four or five months to get over it. That ended up being the major negative side effect until some years later. But due to the operation, I lost at least a third of my respiratory capacity. I have shortness of breath as a result.

My surgery for throat cancer this past summer affected my breathing capacity even more. A couple of doctors told me that such operations were in many ways similar to open-heart surgery. They figure a 10 to 15 percent loss of lung capacity occurs because they have the to break the bronchial tubes, and when they put them back together, they never have that same elasticity. In my case, I think that I had probably 85 or 90 percent capacity before the first lung operation because several years before, my doctor had tested me out on some steps in his office, and my lungs were strong then.

Before my cancer surgery this past summer, my respiratory capacity was at 67 percent. Now I'm down to less than 30 percent. I'm certain that this last operation on my throat was directly necessitated by my smoking. This is so even though I quit seven years ago; quitting was not as hard as I'd expected because I didn't feel I had a choice. I felt that if I didn't quit, I probably would've died, particularly with the reduced lung capacity. It makes it a little easier to quit when the odds are against you. I quit because I was forced to do it if I wanted to live.

Within just a few months after I quit, my senses of smell and taste showed a tremendous difference. It seemed as if my sense of smell got sharper all the time; it was especially nice when we were out in the country. There were some pretty nice smells out there in the spring, and I really noticed them. My sense of taste was sharpened considerably, and I gained some weight, but that was okay because I was recovering from the operation, which had affected my appetite. But after that, I had to watch my weight a little more than before.

Even though quitting was easier than I had anticipated, I did crave cigarettes, but it seemed like each day it was a little better. After about a week, I noticed it was easier day by day. Then every day for months, I used the "one day at a time" game plan. That plan worked really well even though the desire to smoke continued to be pronounced. I think the desire to smoke is a little different than the desire to take a drink. The desire to have a drink kicks in while at a party or while going past a bar, but the desire for nicotine is constant. Taking it one day at a time was a great help to me.

What led up to my last operation felt just like a bad cold I couldn't shake, along with a sore throat that wasn't really very sore. However, I should have taken action faster than I did. And of course, I can't help but blame my family doctor, because I had gone to him months before with this cold in February, and each time I told him my throat was sore, he'd tell me to take some cough medicine. As of late spring, the throat was still sore and I'd get coughing spells, usually in the evening. That lasted for over a month while I still had this slight soreness. I criticize myself severely now for not having gone to another doctor sooner.

In mid-May, I went to an ear, nose, and throat specialist. I told him about my sore throat, and he said it was a little viral infection. Then in early June, I finally went back to my family doctor, and I was ready to scream. I told him, "This sore throat is not going away, and there's something screwy going on with it." He sent me to another specialist. That doctor put a little mirror down my throat and said, "Looks to me like you've got cancer." It was that simple. He said he'd do a biopsy, but if he were a betting man, he'd bet on cancer.

I wasn't really surprised. I kind of expected it. As soon as he said, "I can see something down there," I knew. Before then I had never thought about cancer. In my whole lifetime, I've only known two people who had cancer of the throat. And I've known hundreds of folks who have had other types of cancer.

They operated on me at the beginning of July, when the cancer was pretty far advanced. The first doctor said my whole voice box had to be taken out, but the second one said he could save just a little of it, which he did. But I feel that if I'd started screaming sixty days sooner, it might have turned out differently. I was on the operating table for eight hours. They just had to keep shaving and shaving and shaving on the voice box. I knew my cancer was related to my smoking. I used to think that once you quit, you were safe. I don't believe that anymore. I think if you smoke for fifty years like I did, there's a certain amount of permanent damage. Even though it may not cause cancer in everybody, that's a lot of poison in your system, your throat, your lungs, and other parts of your body.

I came from a big family, one in which many people died of cancer. There were twelve children in my family, and I'm the youngest of six boys. Three girls were younger than me, but my oldest sisters and brothers were twelve to fourteen years older than I was. They all married into other families of ten or twelve children. With all of the marrying and connections to even bigger families, I'm aware of many relatives who died of cancer. I would say in the last five years in this family, there have been at least thirty-five or forty cancer deaths. All my life, I've been aware of the cancer deaths. My brother, who was just older than I was, died at age forty-six with cancer of the lungs. He was a heavy, heavy smoker. He never could quit. He could do anything else, but he couldn't quit. Every time friends or relatives got cancer, I visited them often before they died. I had learned about cancer; one of my cousins died of cancer of the larynx, like mine. And I had a friend, a business acquaintance from about twenty-five years ago, who died. He had his voice box removed. Of all the cancer victims I knew, though, they were the only ones with cancer like mine.

Even though I'd watched relatives and friends die for years, I wasn't inspired to quit. And of course, the older I got, the less need there seemed to be to quit. When you're seventy-two, the actuarial tables are a lot different than when you're twenty-one. Your life expectancy takes on a whole different look. The fear of getting cancer when you're over seventy isn't the same as at fifty or forty. Besides, when you are over seventy, chances are that somewhere in the next twenty years you're going to die anyway.

It's my personal feeling that it's a shame we don't do more educating at the ten-year-old level so that kids never start. My biggest complaint for a long time has been that the Department of Agriculture subsidizes farmers to grow tobacco to kill the American people.

Since my surgery, I've had tremendous difficulty learning how to eat and drink. The eating has been especially hard. It's been ninety days since I had surgery, and I'm still having a lot of difficulty swallowing. I've had to learn to swallow in a new way. And if I'm not careful, I get a tickling in my throat that will throw me into a coughing spell that can really be frightening—I'm not too sure that I'm going to be able to stop sometimes. There have been a couple times that have really scared the heck out of me. Swallowing is hard because to remove the malignant cancer cells, they had to interfere with the windpipe, and the windpipe and the pipe that our food goes down are closely related. We all know what it feels like to get food down our windpipe. That happens a lot after this kind of operation. I have to put my neck way over to one side and try to get the food inside my throat to go down on the side opposite from where the surgery was performed. I don't know how much longer it's going to take to master this.

I still have semiparalysis, a numbness in my ear and my neck and in my tongue, too. All told, it's just the most terrible operation. I hope I'm not going to need radiation because the doctors tell me that there are many nerve cells in your neck and that the first application of radiation kills those nerves. Many of those nerves have to do with the liquefying of a normal amount of mucus that we all develop in our body's systems. The nerves liquefy it, and it goes on through our waste system, but when those nerves are killed, the mucus becomes a solid substance, and it's an awful problem. The threat of pneumonia is multiplied as well.

My voice is gone, even though I can whisper, but my worst problem is my shortness of breath. Even if I still had a full voice box, I would still have shortness of breath. But though my problems are many, I am grateful for the pluses in my life. My sense of smell has improved, and I feel better knowing that I'm in control of something rather than being controlled. That gives me strength.

For decades now, the medical evidence has been overwhelming. There's absolutely no question that smoking damages one's health. When I was a young man, doctors smoked their heads off, but they seldom do that anymore. They see the evidence. It's self-evident that nicotine addiction is harmful. There isn't any benefit to it; and it's tough to break the nicotine habit, but it can be done.

The money saved from not using tobacco, particularly at today's prices, is a benefit. I smoked more than two packs a day for years and years, and that's a pretty expensive habit. And it's a dangerous habit. I can think of many instances where fires were started and there was no question but that they were caused by cigarettes. Smoking is a dirty habit, and it's nice to own my own soul. Not smoking makes me feel good; now I am in charge instead of letting cigarettes rule me. And with all I've lost as a result of smoking, that's important.

Theresa's Story

Theresa, age thirty-seven, is married and the mother of a one-year-old boy.
Trained as a nurse and a family therapist, she is inspired by facilitating mental health
in her family and friends.

I think what interested me most about smoking, what was most significant, was that it was congruent—it felt like it fit with my feelings. When I took a drag off the cigarette that I had lit with a match, it burned and made me feel bad. Then I felt congruent. It felt more real than some other things I had experienced around my home. Smoking fit with the experience of discomfort I had at home. I went for the congruency, and for the altered state. I liked the feeling of being out of control.

I started smoking early, at probably eleven or twelve years of age. It was a way to be with friends. It separated me out with others like me the way basketball or hockey or a writing club might. We had our smoking club. It was a way that we were together. Probably the least scary way to be in a group was to smoke. We just got together and smoked.

I grew up knowing that smoking was an obvious option for my life. This was before the surgeon general's report. It was just another option for being an adult, like drinking coffee. It didn't come with all the moral and health hazard labels it carries now.

Through high school, I smoked off and on due to the availability of time when I could smoke. As soon as it was legal to smoke, when I was eighteen, I was in for a pack and a half a day, and that's where I stayed. It never got more and it never got less. It stayed pretty steady, and I never tried to quit. It never crossed my mind to quit for thirteen years. I quickly entered into the blindness of nicotine addiction. I can remember standing outside at six o'clock in the morning waiting for my ride to nursing school, having had nothing to eat for breakfast, and smoking. It was twenty-five degrees below zero, and I was smoking on the front porch. I couldn't talk. I was having a fit of coughing but continuing to smoke right through it, just getting enough breath to get my next puff on the cigarette.

As I started to have other things that felt congruent in my life, cigarettes felt less and less so. Telling the truth about who I was, and feeling the sweetness of that; and having someone talk back to me honestly and feeling the job of that meant cigarettes filled a need less and less. As those experiences accumulated, then the cloud of denial started to break down. Smoking finally felt less and less compatible with who I was becoming. I was changing. I couldn't smoke in the same way. Finally it no longer fit with how I saw myself.

But the process of quitting took about three years, because of my fear of total withdrawal. I had watched other people quit, and I was living with a nonsmoker. We had certain rules limiting my smoking. I couldn't smoke in the car, and certainly not in the bedroom. My smoking world was contracting. I was overcome by the fear of withdrawal and a lack of faith that I could actually live through the terrors of that process. I was so aware of physical and psychological discomfort that while I tried to quit four or five times, I wasn't successful. Yet I still could not stand the feeling that came as soon as I started to smoke again.

The first time I quit, I tried willpower. I decided I was not going to do it anymore. It was pride. I'd seen my friends quit, so I did it on sheer willpower. I made it about three or four weeks. And then, in a weak moment, I felt angry, or disgusted or something, and I started again. It was hard to do it by willpower.

Several months later, I went through a behavior modification program. I went to groups. It was a psychological conditioning program. I filled out checks for ten dollars each, twenty or more of them. If I broke my commitment to not smoking, I had to send one of the checks to the charity of my choice or whomever I'd made them out to. I was so determined to quit that I made out the checks to my husband's ex-wife, every single check. The program insisted I send them to her, one at a time, with a letter explaining that I had failed in my attempts to quit smoking, and therefore, she was going to gain by my failure. I made it for three or four weeks; then I went to the program instructor and said, "I can't do this. Sending the checks could be serious family trouble for me." I ended up sending the money to something else. So for a second time, I lasted for just a few weeks.

Sometime between three and six weeks, I would just crack. It was never on the first day. It was the continued pressure of the stresses in my life without smoking to lean on. The psychological addiction was pretty much over; the physical addiction remained. My sensations were very much like premenstrual syndrome. I was really irritable, and it felt like I had nerve endings pushing out of my skin. It felt like I was walking through a doorway filled with razor blades and there was only just barely enough room for me to squeeze through. I felt like I was getting little tiny cuts all over my entire body. My whole nervous system was a shambles. Yet again, I went back. It was always around the six-week mark where it was hardest for me. I went back to smoking at least four times when the worst should have already been over.

The next time, I just tried quitting again on my own. My attitude was, okay, now I am going to do it. I started out by trying running. I remember reading someplace about replacing one addiction with another. I thought, I'll run. I got out my little running shoes and started to run. I ran one block, then I had to walk home. I got up to a mile or a mile and a half daily, and it did cut my smoking down. I wouldn't smoke for two hours after I ran. But I gave up running. I was trying all kinds of combinations of things to quit. It got pretty ridiculous.

I would smoke Camels without filters; if I wanted to smoke, that was what I got. Pretty soon I got used to them. I was working nights as a nurse. I remember taking Camels, wrapping the whole package in white surgical tape, the really thick kind, and setting it on the desk. I'd tell the nurse there with me, "I'm not going to smoke tonight, but I'll just leave these here as an option; it'll take me an hour to get to the cigarettes, which will give me time to think about what I'm doing." By three o'clock in the morning, I was having an attack, and I cut through the whole package.

At the time, I was living in a really sleazy place where I would go down to the basement to smoke. I had a chair down there, and any time I wanted to smoke, no matter where I was, I had to go to the basement. That cut me down to three cigarettes a day. Doing it that way helped retrain me for a lifestyle without cigarettes, but I hung onto those three cigarettes and looked forward to them.

I was suffering consequences in my marriage due to smoking. If I had been smoking and my husband wanted to kiss me, I'd do self-conscious stuff. I was self-conscious about my clothes smelling too. Then about eight or nine years ago, after those two or three years of trying, I quit. On this one day, I had been smoking so much that I felt really nauseated, extremely nauseated. I was a student, and between classes, I'd maybe do ten cigarettes before my next class lecture. I thought I was going to throw up, but then I had a flash, almost like a vision, that I had absolutely no control over the cigarettes. I had this vision of these guys who had control of me, in this little college dorm area. I was in a jail cell with cigarettes, totally locked up. They had me handcuffed. I never picked up a cigarette after that. What emerged that day was a flood of insight, a paradigm shift. It felt like a spiritual experience. I had some vacation time, and then Christmas came along right at my critical six-week mark.

I read a lot of autobiographies. I read about scientist Margaret Mead and dancer Isadora Duncan. Reading about other people's lives helped. One morning, I was alone, and I saw a cigarette and lit it. I took one puff. It was so repugnant. It really was as bad as I remembered. It was over. I suddenly realized that I had control over how I felt. That is powerful. And then after that, I got colds. I had respiratory infections for six months. Because of my own struggles, I am empathetic with anyone trying to quit. I feel that smokers are in prison. It is the smelliest habit, and I'm glad for my freedom.

There are so many rewards from not smoking. I can remember walking down the street the first spring after quitting and smelling lilacs before I saw them. That was powerful. I didn't know where they were. I looked around, and they were a little ways away. That felt like a real gift. Before quitting, I had to put flowers right up to my nose before I could smell them. My sensuality changed too; I no longer had that "I need to brush my teeth" feeling. I also discovered that I am a bad cook. I didn't know it before because I couldn't taste the food. I didn't really gain weight, but I did have a shift of metabolism. I didn't have that really scrawny look anymore. I put on about ten pounds, but it made me more solid; it wasn't fat. I've never gotten back to that really skinny look.

One thing I had to learn to do was take breaks. I didn't know how to take breaks—especially on Saturdays. There was nothing built-in to remind me to do it. I would go a whole day and wind up never having really sat down and relaxed. Cigarettes always provided me with what felt like a natural pause, and I had to train myself to take that pause.

My smoking days seem so far away. They seem as far away as the very young woman who was out looking for pot on Friday nights. Bill, my husband, helped me get off nicotine. He neither enabled my smoking nor hassled me about it. He never said anything directly to me about how I should quit, but he would say, "Your smoking is bothering me." How could I argue with that? And he wouldn't say, "Would you mind not smoking?" He said instead, "That is really bothering me. Why don't you put it out?" So it was each cigarette rather than my habit that he confronted. I felt like I had to make those accommodations for him because he was being so honest and personal. He wasn't saying anything about me. He wasn't reproaching me by saying, "It's really bothering me and my air. Why are you doing that?" He just said, "That hurts my lungs." What could I say? I really was good about not smoking around him. If he had come out and directly attacked me, that would have started fires.

I've come to know that smoking is a screen between people. I'm really much more spontaneous now. I don't have to plan for ashtrays or other equipment. I'm freed from that.

Smoking is so vicious. It's a crippling, debilitating addiction. I've learned how really fragile we are. When I see a guy on a lung machine who's still smoking, I understand. I'm always aware that I myself am just one drink or one cigarette away from being crazier than a bedbug. Because of what I've been through, I feel more in common with humanity than separate from it. I have lived through some bad times with both smoking and drinking. I think that with my history, I've sure had some good luck. I'm living on the fuel of that feeling of lucking out, of just missing a trainwreck, because I know I could still be smoking. I would have different friends. I would probably get a new husband. I would organize my life differently.

When it comes to quitting smoking, the replacement factor is a really important element. We must find whatever it is that will keep the spiritual pump going. The Twelve Steps helped me. Taking the leap of faith into the steps, including asking people how they'd quit and then trying to integrate that information so it was useful on my journey, really worked for me. Those Steps seem to help me with everything. The more I get parts of myself into balance, the better my life feels. So when I feel mad, I know I am able to act appropriately, or when I feel sad, or happy. My behavior has started to have some appropriateness; my perceptions now better match my environment. When I feel paranoid, it's because I am in a dark alley, so to speak. I think working the Steps leads to inner harmony—to congruency.

Being smoke-free positively affects relationships, especially for women. I don't know if it has that effect so much for men. For most women, relationships are so integral and have such a high value in our lives. It's harder and harder to smoke when we know that smoking is a screen. To get through my withdrawal, I tapped into my faith that I really would come out on the other side. The other five times I tried to quit, I didn't have faith.

I believe there are people who will go right to their end smoking, and that it's not their fault because it's not willpower, nor is it because they didn't work the Steps in the right way. I think maybe it's just fate. More and more, I believe in some kind of "recycling" process, not reincarnation exactly, but some process that makes some sense of why people go through their lives not having the blessings others have. Why can some people quit only when they are seventy, while some, like my dad, quit at sixty, and why did I escape nicotine when I was thirty? It's hard to explain. It seems that all of us are given the choice to make the best of our opportunities. Some of us will accomplish it. That's my philosophy in a nutshell.

Kathy's Story

Kathy, age forty-six, is a divorced mother of four (now ages seventeen to twenty-six).
She works in real estate and loves tennis, people, traveling, and art history.

I don't remember my very first cigarette, but I do remember that I was about fifteen. My dad smoked Salems and Camels, and he kept them in a drawer in a buffet. My brother Joe and I used to steal a few and go smoke them out behind the garage. Because I hated Salems, I began to buy my own cigarettes. First I smoked Pall Malls, and then somewhere along the way the Marlboro man got to me. It got to be cool to smoke Marlboros.

I really liked smoking, and it seemed everybody did it. for sure all my friends did. In actuality, probably a lot of kids didn't smoke. Everybody tried it, but not everyone kept it up. At slumber parties, if one person had a pack of cigarettes, everybody smoked, but not everybody started buying them after that.

My sister Rita was one of the kids who didn't smoke. We shared a third-floor bedroom, and I can remember sitting and smoking, blowing the smoke out the window and threatening her with decapitation if she told on me. Even though I smoked with regularity, I never smoked around my parents until after I got married. (I may even have had my first child before I smoked in front of them, even though they both smoked.) I was afraid they would shame me for smoking, so I didn't risk it. I didn't swear around my parents either. I didn't do anything around my parents except be absolutely darling. It was my little sisters who got to be brats. I guess I was terrified that they would abandon me or something, so I was always on my good behavior.

I can recall when I made the decision that I was old enough to smoke in front of my mother. I remember actually lighting up at her house and feeling both defiant and self-conscious, but nothing really happened. There weren't any negative repercussions. I was twenty or twenty-one by that time.

I enjoyed smoking. I loved it from the very first time. When I was about twenty-one or twenty-two and pregnant with my second child, I tried to quit smoking and realized then that I was hooked. I couldn't quit, and that surprised me. I hadn't tried to quit because I was pregnant, I just decided to quit; however, I can remember making the decision not to quit after all. It was a Saturday, and my husband was at work. By four o'clock in the afternoon, I was in tough shape. I was really impatient with my year-and-a-half-old daughter because I was crazy from withdrawal. I needed a cigarette badly. We had only one car, so I had to wait for Tom to get home. When he got back, I was sitting on the front step with our daughter Chris, and I jumped in the car, drove to the store, and bought a pack of cigarettes. That was the first time I was ever aware that I couldn't quit just anytime I wanted.

I tried to quit a few more times after that due to the consequences smoking was causing in my life. I burned holes in clothes and furniture. Oftentimes it was because I'd drink too much. I remember one time burning a hole in a gorgeous, brand-new dress when I was drunk. It never occurred to me to quit drinking, but I did try to quit smoking several times. I'd never last more than a day without nicotine, and then I'd decide the hole wasn't *that* bad and I'd go buy a pack of cigarettes. I continued to smoke pretty consistently for the next twenty years.

Early in my smoking history, I was confronted by the tragic effects of nicotine addiction because my mother-in-law had cancer and her doctors made her quit smoking. She even had to have a breast removed. Yet neither my husband nor my mother-in-law suggested I quit. But there was no consciousness about it back then—the whole awareness of tobacco's real dangers was low at that time. And back then, almost everybody I associated with smoked: my whole family, including my parents, and friends as well, except for my husband. Actually I was surprised recently to read statistics that showed only one-third of the population smoked. I figured it was the other way around.

Even though I had quit for a day here and there many times, I never seriously worked on quitting until after I was divorced and in a new relationship with a man who hated smoking. I was terrified that if I smoked in front of him, he would abandon me. That was my direct motivation to quit.

Also, at the time, I had a neighbor who had a really husky voice. Her doctor had been after her for years to quit smoking. She even had polyps on her throat. That motivated me too. Additionally, I was influenced by a friend and traveling companion who was allergic to cigarette smoke. Our agreement always was that I'd never smoke in our room when we were on a trip together. Normally that worked out okay because we would travel to places that were warm, like Florida or Mexico, where I could go out on the balcony to smoke. So my smoking was never really a problem, not until we planned a thirty-day trip to Europe in January, when it was going to be cold. I knew I was going to be feeling really resentful about having to go down to the lobby of the hotel or out in a hallway or somewhere to smoke. I loved traveling with her, and I really loved our friendship. I didn't want to feel resentful. I knew I'd have to quit smoking to go on the trip or else I'd end up hating her. Fortunately, while planning the trip, I got more heavily involved with John and decided to quit even before confirming the trip departure. But it wasn't easy.

It was awful. And every time I've quit, it's gotten worse. The withdrawal is absolutely horrible. The first three days are horrible, and then the ninth, tenth, and eleventh days are extremely hard again, and then at six weeks, it's terrible once more. At the time, one of my sisters was quitting too. We were going to college together, and we'd sit in the smoking room and smoke, and then she'd eat a whole tube of toothpaste before she'd go home and see her husband. She told me it's normal to grieve the loss of cigarettes and that the sixth week, the sixth month, and then anniversary dates are the hardest times in the grieving process. If you're aware of that beforehand, you can watch out for those times and get over the humps.

The second time I quit, it was really hard for me too around the six-week mark. But I continued to miss cigarettes in general anyway, no matter how long I had been off them. Today is my seventeenth month anniversary of quitting smoking, and that's the longest I've ever gone without a cigarette since I began. Fourteen and a half months was the longest I had ever stayed off tobacco prior to this time. But I still miss cigarettes, not all the time, but occasionally.

Each time, my approach to quitting was to try to tough it out, but the rewards of doing that have never been particularly great. I know it's a delusional perception, but it seems my consequences for smoking were not as severe as they are for not smoking. While smoking, I'd have less wind on the tennis court, but since quitting smoking, I've gained so much weight that I have as much trouble getting around a tennis court as I did forty pounds ago, when I was smoking a pack and a half of cigarettes a day. My lungs are pinker, but my rewards for being a nonsmoker are not feeling that great.

When I quit the time before this one and went fourteen and a half months smoke-free, I missed smoking every single day. Finally, one day I called up my sister and told her I was going to start smoking again. I asked her if she would still love me, and she told me, "Yes." She suggested I wait a few hours before going out to buy cigarettes. I did, but I went out and bought cigarettes anyway. This was during a period of my life when I was trying to control my drinking. After two or three weeks of sobriety, I would slip into drinking every once in a while, and I believed that if I allowed myself to smoke, it would be easier to quit drinking. Of course that wasn't true. I felt ashamed for having let people down. Some good friends had been really supportive of my not smoking. My traveling companion used to bring me flowers on my monthly anniversaries. She had been so excited when I quit smoking. She was really disappointed. It was easy to feel defensive, but I was manufacturing the shame. Nobody shamed me, but I managed to feel it anyway.

I smoked again for about two and a half years. And then I started going out with another man who didn't smoke. One night, we were playing Trivial Pursuit with a crowd, and I was the only smoker. I felt really uncomfortable, and that night was the last time I smoked. By then, I was sober too. I'd been going to A.A. meetings for a year and a half, and I hadn't had a drink for about six or eight months. But in the meantime, I had skin cancer. The doctor kept telling me to quit smoking. He said he'd rather I expose my body to the heaviest mega-rays of sun for the rest of my life than smoke. He went on to tell me that while he could carve skin cancer out of me for ever and ever and ever, he couldn't carve my lungs out. That scared me, but not enough to make me quit right away.

Finally, the combination of the information, my past experience, and a love interest who didn't smoke gave me the strength to quit again, but it was total insanity. I was going to real estate school, and it was pretty stressful. I'd been out of college for a while, and there I was, sitting in classes and taking tests while in withdrawal. To this day I can't believe I survived that without smoking. I quit smoking on a Tuesday and took the real estate licensing exam on Saturday. I studied, and I prayed, "God, if You intend for me to be a nonsmoker, help me to pass this test." But I couldn't concentrate. My concentration was totally gone. I could barely get through a *People* magazine. I couldn't even watch television or read. When I discovered I could now get all the way through a *People* magazine without jumping up off the couch five hundred times, I knew I was making progress.

I just couldn't sit still. I was in constant motion, mostly from my chair in the living room to the refrigerator. One of the reasons I'd always started smoking again after quitting previously was because I was gaining so much weight. Before going into treatment for alcoholism, I gained thirty pounds. I went into treatment as a nonsmoker and started smoking about two weeks later. I couldn't deal with all the pain going on inside me, and everybody there smoked. I really didn't want to start smoking again, but I was so preoccupied with it. One of the counselors said the decision to start again was between me and my Higher Power. I went right back to my room and took a pack of my roommates' cigarettes and started smoking. The thirty pounds I'd gained haunted me, and I was desperate to lose the weight. Every time I tried to diet, I'd go crazy. I'd just crawl out of my skin. At that time, going back to smoking was actually helpful. I was able to stay on a diet and not feel like I was going to crawl out of my skin.

What I now know is that nicotine is a mood-altering chemical that was keeping my fear level manageable. So once again I smoked for fourteen months, and I loved every minute of it, knowing full well that I was going to quit again someday when I got a little more time in sobriety. My A.A. sponsor also really encouraged me to get some more sobriety and to trust that when I was ready to quit, I would know it. And that was what I did.

I was surprised when I actually quit. A friend of mine had just been diagnosed with lung cancer. He was my age, and he had only months to live. I was going on a trip the day I heard about his diagnosis, and I made a decision to quit when I got home from my trip. But I didn't even wait until I got home. The day that I started my journey to return home, I quit. I went out that morning to play tennis at about eleven o'clock, and I couldn't even see the ball. Withdrawal had set in. But I was done. I sat in the no-smoking section on my flight home, and I haven't had a cigarette since.

I had been through quitting attempts a lot of times before, so I knew what to expect, but it was even worse than I remembered. Fortunately, a friend spoon-fed me a lot of good information. She'd quit about three months earlier. I received the insights of her personal program on a one-to-one basis. It was really nice; and beyond that, it was helpful. She would tell me what was happening to me physically. She had a medical background and explained how nicotine was a toxin—a poison—and that was why my body was just crawling with discomfort.

She really held my hand throughout the process. Another woman my age who had quit several months before also really supported me as well. And I swam every day, sometimes two or three times a day. I took a lot of whirlpool soaks and bubble baths during that first three or four days. And I went for a massage every other day for the first week, plus I didn't eat sugar. The first three days were really horrible. My ears rang. My skin crawled. I felt like I was going to come right out of my skin. It was a terrible withdrawal.

Having people around, telling me that it would get better, helped. The other thing that really helped a lot was reading my daily meditation books and substituting the word "cigarettes" for "alcohol." And I used affirmations over and over and over again. I truly believed in my heart that God's will for me was that I would be a nonsmoker. I had gone to an effective living seminar three or four years earlier where they taught us how to use affirmations for more successful living. They had very specifically suggested that if you are still smoking and would like to be a nonsmoker, you could create affirmations about being a nonsmoker and repeat them daily. Their theory was that your subconscious doesn't know the difference between past, present, and future. It can only hear what it is given. It doesn't act on it in any kind of specific time frame. I used my nonsmoking affirmations for two or three months, even before I actually quit smoking. That, along with my friend's death, may have been the catalyst. At any rate, one day I knew I was done with smoking.

For me, the second phase of not smoking is a craving for tobacco that's really tied in with my addiction to sugar. When I go on a sugar binge, my thinking gets all screwed up and I get stronger nicotine withdrawal symptoms. I would rationalize that if I could smoke, the sugar withdrawal sensations would go away. Sugar binging causes the crawling skin, the ringing ears, and an inability to deal with reality—all the same symptoms that come with nicotine withdrawal. I don't understand it, but as I sit in my bed, I know that if I smoke, my discomfort will go away. Instead, I choose to go to the supermarket and buy donuts or something.

My struggle may never be over. Just the other day my cravings hit. I left work; I was parked in the underground garage. I came off the elevator and could immediately tell someone had been smoking in the hallway. When I smelled the cigarette smoke, I had a euphoric memory of how I loved smoking. By the time I got to my car (which was maybe a hundred feet from where I'd smelled the cigarette smoke), I had already thought about stopping at the SuperAmerica store near work to buy a pack of cigarettes. I didn't smoke in my brand-new car, but I figured I could just smoke a cigarette kind of, like around the edges, just smoke a half of one and then throw it away. The first one doesn't taste very good anyway. In my fantasy, I figured that when I got home, I could hide them from my daughter. I knew she was working. I figured I could quit the next day. I knew it would be really painful, but I could do it. I hadn't even reached my car and this whole scenario had gone through my head. It really hit me just what an addict I really am. I don't even want to smoke, but that's just how quickly the craving for it can hit.

In order to quit, I really needed the affirmations for strength. I still use them. The one I use the most is: "God's will for me is that I am a nonsmoker." I truly believe in that affirmation, and it feels good. It was probably the first real and directly conscious contact with a Higher Power I've ever had in all the years I've been in a Twelve Step program. I also used an affirmation about abundance. This one still helps me when I get into abusing food by overeating: "There's abundance in the world, and I have more than enough." This affirmation has to do with filling the inner hole that smoking or food or whatever takes care of.

After seventeen months and lots of struggle, I'm really glad I'm a nonsmoker, mostly because it gets more and more difficult all the time to smoke and enjoy it. I was at a brunch recently with seventeen women, and there were two smokers there but no ashtrays! It just wasn't acceptable to smoke. More and more people want their homes to be smoke-free.

Being the only smoker even at a restaurant with eight people is not easy either. I'm really glad that I don't have to put up with that anymore. It feels good to go someplace for four or five hours and not have to leave because I need to go smoke. I no longer have to stand around with all the icky people at a party because they're surrounding the only ashtray.

And I assume I am getting healthier, although I don't necessarily feel better yet physically. It's wonderful to wake up in the morning without that terrible taste in my mouth. I only noticed that change in the first few weeks after quitting; since then, I no longer remember what the terrible taste is like. I forget what cigarette hangovers were like, too. It's nice not to have them, but I don't think about it very often.

I've gained forty pounds, and it really hard not to focus on it as a direct result of becoming a nonsmoker. But the reality is that I have a problem with substance abuse, and right now, my substance is food. I joined a group for food substance abusers last week, and that feels good. I think I'm on the homestretch.

I know that now I'm a nonsmoker forever. I still think about smoking, though, whenever I feel agitation. Whenever I have anxiety going on, I want to smoke because it used to take down my anxiety level. But I can't think of anything that would make me so anxious that I would believe smoking would be necessary to cure it. I have other ways to deal with my anxieties now.

PART III

Meditations

Strength Through Meditation: Ninety Daily Meditations

The stories you have just read were told to me by men and women like yourself. These are men and women for whom taking on the struggle to give up nicotine in order to become their better selves was not an easy decision. Nor was it easy to remain loyal to this commitment. All of them admitted they needed support from friends or a Higher Power or both in order to get through the unexpectedly difficult days or particularly trying circumstances that arose. Each of them might have found the struggle less difficult had they been able to read and contemplate the series of meditations that follow.

Millions of people, specifically those who enjoy the support and friendship offered in Twelve Step programs like Alcoholics Anonymous, Al-Anon, and Narcotics Anonymous,[1] have grown to love and depend on the spiritual guidance offered in daily meditation books.

The purpose of these books[2] is to offer quiet and very personal support, as well as insight and hope, to the individual who really wants a better life. The following ninety meditations are offered for this same purpose.

I settled on a series of ninety meditations because most people find the first three months after quitting nicotine the most difficult. And it's during these first three months that we're most vulnerable. It's imperative we remember we're only a cigarette away from being ensnared once again in the clutches of tobacco. Having a brief passage to read when we're feeling insecure about

---

1   There are over a hundred different kinds of Twelve Step programs active at present throughout the world.

2   These books include *Twenty-Four Hours a Day, Each Day a New Beginning, The Promise of a New Day, Touchstones,* and *Night Light.*

our resolve not to smoke will get us over the hump, beyond the urge to smoke. We can quietly turn to the same meditation or a different one as many times as we'd like throughout the day. The urges will pass, I promise you. And the meditations will offer strength; this, too, I promise you.

If you are still not as comfortable as a nonsmoker as you had hoped for at the end of ninety days, begin again with reading day one. Many of us who read other daily meditation books read and reread the same books throughout a lifetime. Each day, a meditation we've read many times before will offer us new insight and additional strength because we will have grown and changed since our last reading of it.

The quotes introducing each meditation were spoken to me by people who were interviewed. They inspired my thoughts as I wrote the meditations. It's my prayer that you will find comfort, guidance, strength, and most of all, hope in the days ahead by reading the pages that follow. Remember, whatever our goal happens to be, all of us need support to meet with success. Let the meditations give you that support. Let them carry you forward to the triumph that awaits you.

Day 1

"I don't have to quit forever.
I can go back and use tobacco tomorrow if I want to;
all I have to do is just not use it today."

We can do anything for this one day. Nothing will be too much for us. We can even break the day down into each of its twenty-four hours if the struggle demands it. We can then focus on just one hour at a time. Assuredly, we can survive sixty minutes at a time without cigarettes. How freeing it is to realize we only have to quit smoking for today.

It's helpful to remember all we are ever guaranteed is the present. We can hope for a fruitful future. And most likely it will come to pass; however, each time we give our attention to "when" rather than to the present, we're missing the richness of the tapestry our experiences are weaving right now.

Our decision to not smoke today, coupled with both the pain and the glory of our choice, will add to the meaning and beauty of our tapestry. Today is our gift from the Creator. How we live these twenty-four hours is our gift in return.

I will do whatever I need to do to live without a cigarette today.
It's all the life I'm certain of.

Day 2

"I realized I really was powerless and trusted that if other people could do it, so could I."

Nicotine is powerful, so powerful. It has had me in its grip for a long time, and it doesn't easily let go. My compulsion to smoke can't be controlled, and it haunts me. but the decision to give in to the compulsion is controllable—by me, every time it comes. I am only powerless over the desire, not the decision to smoke.

My struggle to live without tobacco feels lonely and painful, but millions have survived it before, and millions are living through it with me today. I am strengthened by knowing we share these moments in time. We are bonded even though we are often strangers to one another.

**I feel stronger just knowing I'm sharing this struggle
with a friend I'll never meet.**

Day 3

---

*"I can manage the withdrawal. It will come,
and I trust it will go away."*

Every moment has its time. Pleasurable moments with a friend as well as painful moments because of hurt feelings pass very quickly. I must remember the adage "this too shall pass" when the desire to smoke again clouds my thoughts and disrupts my actions.

The moments that herald the euphoric recall of a day's first cigarette are just as fleeting as the moments I'll spend at a stop sign or making a phone call today. Time passes on. I can't stop it, nor does it wait for me. My desire to smoke today will pass because its moment will pass. All I have to do is give my attention to the next moment as it signals me.

**I can live through today's collection of moments
without tobacco.**

Day 4

---

*"One problem is I don't ask for help
when I want a cigarette."*

Why do I think I must do everything alone? Am I ashamed to say I need help? Am I afraid I'll look weak if I admit how very hard it is to quit?

No smoker finds it easy to quit. Some do it without much fanfare, but not without some inner struggle. It's much better to get support from friends and coworkers who will want to help us stay committed to our decision to stop.

Whenever we share ourselves freely with someone else, particularly when we're revealing how vulnerable we are, or how the present struggle is difficult, we'll know a new freedom and a new closeness to the friend who has listened. Everyone likes to offer help; when we ask for help during these difficult times, we're doing something valuable for two people—ourselves and the one whom we ask.

**Let me remember that my asking for help today
is a gift to someone else, too.**

Day 5

---

*"Just one day is all I have to quit for,
and they'll add up."*

There is no doubt we can do anything asked of us and survive any hardship for just one day. And what a good fortune that this is all our Higher Power has ever expected of us. Little by little, our experiences unfold by design—in a way that is all the better for us to learn our lessons.

Quitting smoking is just another unfolding experience, and we have only today to focus on. No matter how enticing a cigarette may seem, regardless of the depth of our longing, we can abstain today. And tomorrow will take care of itself.

For many of us, past attempts at quitting were thwarted because we envisioned years of tomorrows, feeling deprived of the comfort we sought from cigarettes. How helpful it is to quiet our minds to the future. It isn't here now. Only today is here—twenty-four short hours, a mere flash. Surely we can survive a mere flash without a cigarette.

**I'll look at today—only today, and I know I can live
without smoking.**

Day 6

"For most people, quitting is not just black and white;
for most people, it's a series of stopping and starting
and stopping again."

The decision to quit must be renewed daily. It's hard to give us the friend who comforted us when we were scared or sad—who never deserted us when we were lonely, keeping us company during a long evening at home or on the road traveling.

Let's not ignore our grief. It's normal and healthy to grieve the loss of something that was as close as our breath. But let's also remember cigarettes were dangerous friends; our personal welfare was forever at stake while in their company.

One day at a time, or even one hour at a time, is all we need to concern ourselves with. Let's decide now, for the rest of today only, that we will not smoke. Our tomorrows will take care of themselves.

It will strengthen me to recommit myself to this decision every day. Twenty-four hours is such a short span in contrast to all that has gone before.

Day 7

*"It's wonderful not being in conflict
with my values anymore."*

For a long time I didn't want to smoke, and yet I did. I'd feel ashamed I couldn't just quit. At night I'd resolve to quit, but start again the next morning. What a relief it is knowing I'm not unique.

Values are what guide our thoughts and actions. When we're in conflict with our values, we feel self-conscious and ill-at-ease. Values can't be ignored, though we try to pretend otherwise. Pain and shame are frequent reminders that our values are alive and demand our attention.

If I decide to smoke again, my values will torment me, and I can't quiet them. But I can make the right decision about how I'll live my life today, a decision that promises peacefulness throughout my being.

My values love me, sometimes more than I love myself.

Stop Smoking and Vaping Now!

Day 8

***

*"I started doing some imaging
of myself as a nonsmoker."*

Our minds are so powerful. We can prepare ourselves for a challenge by visualizing ourselves gracefully surviving it. We can get help for working through a tense situation with a friend or foe by imaging the encounter in a positive light. Imaging how we might handle any experience in a detailed way will give us the courage and the strength to tackle whatever confronts us.

Using imagery will deepen our commitment to being a nonsmoker. In time, we'll not be able to imagine we ever smoked. However, in the meantime, we'll be helped by systematically spending some time alone, quietly meditating on the image of ourselves going through the hours of the day, happily acting out our part without the hindrance of a cigarette.

Imagery works because it can make something we haven't yet experienced seem familiar. It teaches us how to act in the experience visualized. We quickly become 'old hands' because our minds have made us experienced.

**My experience as a nonsmoker will be enhanced
by a few moments of imagery today.**

Day 9

---

*"I would buy a pack of cigarettes and smoke two.
And then I'd stand over the toilet and rip them all
up and flush the toilet. And then the next day I'd do
something similar."*

Tobacco's power is awesome when we give in to it. We all have memories, strong and awful memories of behavior for which we feel shame. Maybe it's digging through trash for a cigarette butt that's only long enough for one puff, or stealing change from a child's piggy bank for that late night trek to the all-night store for a needed smoke.

Today, we want freedom from the pull of tobacco. That's why we're here now. We want to be in charge of our own lives, of our own decisions regarding time, money, health, and activities. If we're smoking, we're not in charge. Tobacco is king, and we're only its subjects, bowing to its many demands.

**I don't have to create more awful memories for myself today.
Rather, I can create ones that will continue to give me hope
and strength.**

Day 10

"Quitting smoking and quitting drinking are just the first steps for me. I feel excited about my future at last."

Each day stretches before us, awaiting our involvement. Whether we approach our activities at work or home with enthusiasm or dread depends on the attitude we've cultivated. Attitudes don't just happen; they are honed ever so carefully, and they are nourished by us every moment.

When we've made a radical change in our lives, one that we know nourishes us beneficially, it lends an air of excitement to our perception of the activities that lie ahead of us. The future can always excite us. And it will, as long as we are committed to being the people we really want to be., and remain open to the adventure each day promises.

Becoming a nonsmoker is our chance to be the person we long to be. New doors will open to new opportunities because we have closed the door on the self who controlled us in years past. All of life—play, work, friends, talents, and dreams—will take on a new appearance now that we can see with a clearer vision.

Not smoking has changed how everything looks to me. It's almost like being reborn. Life feels fresh, like the air in early spring.

Day 11

*"I am changing my patterns. I'm taking control.
The nicotine is no longer in control, and that feels good."*

There are so many activities we thought we'd never be able to do without an accompanying cigarette. Most of us were convinced smoking helped us think, relax, write, and converse. We probably relied on cigarettes when we were lonely and afraid. And now there's genuine joy in the discovery that we can get through the stressful tasks as well as the boring everyday chores that demand our attention during our day without the assistance of a cigarette.

Making changes in our lives, changes we're certain are beneficial to us in the present as well as the future, feels really good. we do have the power and the responsibility for our personal development. We have always had them, but in many instances, we didn't make good decisions about our behavior. However, quitting smoking has given us a very strong taste of self-determination in action, and it's exhilarating.

We'll discover as time goes on that it will get increasingly easier to make other healthy choices for ourselves. And each beneficial choice we make will strengthen us for the next.

I can do anything asked of me today without a cigarette.

Day 12

"If I'm in a certain situation where I know I would have smoked in the past, I'm removing myself from that situation."

The memories of how, when, and where we smoked are terrifically powerful, particularly in the early weeks of our abstinence. Memories tug at us, grabbing our attention; they tempt us, and they distract us from reality. We can't trust the fond recall of cigarettes over cups of coffee. The real truths—the coughing and congestion, the stains and burns on our bodies and clothes, the frequent searches for leftover butts long enough to smoke—are too easily hidden from our thoughts.

Fortunately, by exercising choice, we can avoid certain people, situations, or activities that seemed to compel us to smoke in the past. We need not stay anywhere that doesn't nurture our new identity. We should only spend time with people and frequent places that will lovingly nurture our developing self. Each time we leave a setting that tempts us to smoke again, we'll grow in strength and self-esteem.

**If I don't want to slip into my old habits,
I'll avoid the slippery places today.**

Day 13

"I feel better knowing I'm in control of something rather than being controlled. That gives me strength."

We can't control the weather, other people, nor the outcome of most situations; but we can control our own behavior and attitudes. We can either be contented nonsmokers or frustrated, nervous, and disgruntled ones. The choice is ours. The ability to control our thoughts and actions exists solely within ourselves; it's empowering to know we are in control of how we will behave today.

No friend or stranger in our path today can make us act against our will. We might be tempted to lash out, to feel shame, or to be intimidated by another's behavior. But how we can respond to any situation is totally within our own control. It's an awesome responsibility taking charge of our lives—owning our behavior. And it's also inspiring and exhilarating.

I'm not smoking today because I am choosing this path for me.
It's my decision and my life; I'm in charge!

Day 14

---

*"When the urge to smoke surfaces,
I recognize it and let it pass."*

Approximately every eight minutes, a smoker's body cries out for nicotine; and within minutes, the craving is generally satisfied. We should not be surprised that our bodies are experiencing torment and letting us know about it. Nicotine is a demanding and deadly drug, and it expects to imprison us once again. A strong urge is nicotine's bait.

We have some tools to handle the urges so they need not overwhelm us. We can very simply replace the thought with one that's more beneficial to us. We are the creators of all our thoughts. Negative thoughts don't happen to us—we give them birth.

We can develop the skill of imaging, and in our mind's eye, we can learn to see a picture of us contentedly going about our daily affairs smoke-free. We can also turn to others who like us are opting for a healthier life without cigarettes. Support is always available. And finally, we each have a Higher Power who comforts, guides, and eases our path when we're on the right track.

I am on the right track today. I'll let all the forces help me stay on this path.

Day 15

---

*"This last time I quit, it was easier because I wanted
to quit. I didn't have the leftover feeling
that I ought to quit."*

Relapse has been a reality for many of us. Nicotine is a formidable drug, and it gives us a tough battle. If it's a battle we've lost in the past, perhaps it's because we were trying to quit for someone else or because we entered the fight alone, without the support or strength available to us from our Higher Power or our network of friends and other nonsmokers.

We don't ever have to rely solely on our own resources to accomplish any goal, to shift our perceptions, or to make a major change in our lives. Our own resources are seldom enough. They are strengthened many times over when we team them with the strength of friends who want us to succeed and with a Higher Power that is loving. This decision not to smoke is no harder than we make it.

**I can set the intention to look within myself and to others
to help me adhere to my decision today.**

Day 16

---

*"Right now I still feel out of control
because I'm not smoking."*

Tobacco was the object of our attention: buying it, stashing it, hoarding it, using it, and even on occasion hiding it. We were in control over our relationship with tobacco, which provided us with a false sense of security. Our need to feel in control of something—situations, personal achievements, other people—is immense and yet is thwarted on most occasions. Tobacco filled the need for control, and now that's gone.

Our decision to quit smoking is giving us an opportunity to recognize the emptiness of false security. One lesson is that the only control that rests completely with us is the control we exert over our own behavior and attitudes.

There's another lesson if we want to explore it—it's a spiritual lesson. It rests with our acknowledgment of a greater power within us, a power that will guide our behaviors and soften our attitudes. Turning to the power within will offer us the security we longed for from tobacco.

**Today will be restful and productive
if I turn within for security.**

Day 17

"Since I quit smoking, I can't concentrate."

It's not unusual to be obsessed with the desire to smoke. Smoking was a key part of nearly every activity in our life before. When a best friend moves away, our thoughts are drawn to that person often. A gentle reminder to return our attention to the present is really all that's necessary, but let's not be surprised by the frequency of this necessity.

How resilient human beings are. There's very little we can't recover from. And we can recover from smoking. Problem-solving may be harder for a while. A well-written novel may not captivate us. Even a scintillating conversation may lose our attention—but time is very healing.

If we truly desire freedom from our addiction to tobacco, we must be patient with ourselves. The obsession with smoking will leave us. Our ability to concentrate will return without the distraction that accompanied smoking.

**I'll not dwell on my hunger for cigarettes today.
It's merely a thought, and I'm in charge of my thoughts.**

Stop Smoking and Vaping Now!

Day 18

"I feel good about myself for being able to stay away from cigarettes for twenty-two years."

Even one day without cigarettes feels like a milestone when we first quit. And it is! We deserve congratulations for our efforts. It's appropriate for us to share our success with someone who can both understand our struggle and give us support.

Remember, we have only one day at a time to not smoke. We can make the decision anew tomorrow. Today is all we have. Perhaps someday we'll also have twenty-two years of one days of not smoking. But for now, there isn't any experience we can't survive, even the torment of no cigarette, for this one day.

At today's end, how proud and grateful we'll feel about not succumbing to the frequent urges to smoke. The people who quit for one or ten or twenty-two years aren't endowed with any special characteristics. They are just like ourselves, but they're more comfortable with their choice to not smoke.

I can easily handle today without a cigarette if I rely on my inner strength and the support of well-wishers.

Day 19

"Everybody becomes a nonsmoker during the night."

Tackling the challenge of giving up cigarettes seemed monumental at first, until we were reminded that we survived six to eight hours every night with no nicotine. True, those hours were uncluttered with the tension of deadlines or angry people or unfamiliar situations. But the important point is we have survived years of nighttimes without smoking. It's a fact worth celebrating.

When the urge to resume the habit tempts us, it's encouraging to remember those accumulated hours of not smoking. Any technique we can employ to strengthen our commitment is well worth the effort. Let's be mindful that there are very few activities more harmful to ourselves, as well as to those forced to experience our polluted air, than smoking.

Let's live these next twenty-four hours one at a time, as willing nonsmokers. The eight or so hours we're asleep will take care of themselves, leaving only sixteen for us to be in charge of. One hour at a time is manageable.

I can easily handle a sixty-minute time segment, and it's really pretty easy to string a few of them together.

Day 20

"Since quitting, I've felt like I'm in a honeymoon period. I'm really positive."

Taking charge of our lives—whether through a new job, leaving a bad relationship, or changing our eating or drinking habits—is a guaranteed way to boost our self-esteem. Each time we follow through on a decision destined to benefit us either spiritually, physically, or emotionally, we find instantaneous gratification. We are learning that quitting smoking offers just such gratification.

Though it's not easy for all of us to do, saying no to tobacco in this moment feels good and right because we are taking back our personal power. Nicotine no longer controls our thoughts, our attitudes, our behavior. We are discovering just how much time we devoted to smoking. The irony is that smoking not only took minutes and hours away from life's activities, but months, perhaps years, from our expected life span. Tobacco in any form is double jeopardy.

**I look in the mirror today and I feel great.
I'm excited about taking charge of my behavior.**

Day 21

"It's really special to find I care enough about myself that I don't want to kill myself."

For many years, most of us have been in a state of denial about the harmful effects of cigarettes. Physical problems have even been evident for some of us, but we shook off the reality of their impact. Yet here we are. At last! To the relief of family and friends, we are living one day at a time without nicotine.

It wasn't an easy decision to give up our crutch; smoking had coaxed us through many long nights and troubling experiences. But our return had diminished greatly: Nicotine eventually takes its toll on every user because users become abusers, and few—ever so few—are social smokers. It seems there's an addict lurking in everybody. Our drug of choice varies, that's all.

Even though we're in the early phases of freedom from nicotine, it's essential to congratulate ourselves for opting to live rather than participating in a slow, passive death. We have many brothers and sisters who need the benefit of our example.

It's never too early to congratulate myself on my progress.

Day 22

"Whenever the urge to smoke came over me the first few days, I used a little mental trick of pretending I was between cigarettes."

There are thousands of techniques we can use to support our efforts not to smoke, and we should not shy away from any of them. Nobody finds stopping easy; we often have to give ourselves permission to be honest about the difficulty we're experiencing.

Too many of us grew up with the advice, "Be tough. It's weak to need help." The reality is that asking for help strengthens rather than weakens us, and the people we ask for help are strengthened as well. Shared vulnerability enhances the spiritual development of all who are privy to the sharing.

Imaging ourselves as healthy, happy, contented nonsmokers helps to reprogram the subconscious, so it's a valuable tool in our reeducation process. Simply acknowledging each urge and letting it pass can also become a useful and easy habit to develop. Let's not forget that we are the makers of our thoughts. We can replace any urge with whatever thought we prefer.

I'm the master of my mind for all of the twenty-four hours ahead of me.

Day 23

"I intentionally carried a pack of cigarettes around with me the whole day because I wanted to make it clear to myself that what I was doing was by choice."

Accepting responsibility for who we are and the progress we've made with our lives is a sign of maturity. It's far easier to blame parents or bosses or "the system" for our struggles and failings.

Quitting smoking is a mature act because it's a choice we've made for ourselves. For most of us, it took a great deal of thought and preparation. Perhaps others encouraged us, and their continuing support will strengthen us; but we are on our own and must be fully accountable only to ourselves.

Not smoking is a major change in our lives; smoking was our companion in virtually every activity that engaged us. We'll feel abandoned for a time. Our attention span will be intermittent for a while. Our patience and tolerance will likely be tested. But more importantly, our health—emotionally, physically, and spiritually—will be enhanced. We'd do well to focus on these positive aspects.

**As a nonsmoker, I'm guaranteed a healthier life.
I'll work on my gladness today.**

Day 24

"I feel such a sense of emotional loss whenever I quit."

Smoking has comforted me. It's been a very attentive friend, always softening my sadness and relieving my loneliness. I feel naked, frustrated, empty, and edgy without a cigarette to rely on. I can't expect these first few days to be easy. And it's okay to grieve the loss of my companion.

Surviving the first cup of coffee; the first meal; the first phone call, the first major argument, the first weekend, and the first good cry without a cigarette will give me the strength needed to survive other difficult times. We can keep track of our milestones as we complete them, and our resourcefulness and our resolve will grow. Each moment without a cigarette is helping me become a person with a future of choices I hadn't dreamed of before.

The loss I feel today will pass, of that I'm certain.

Day 25

---

*"Smoking isn't handsome or beautiful or sophisticated.
It's a lie to believe otherwise."*

As a teenager, I was fully convinced that dangling a cigarette from my mouth made me appear sexy. I wanted to be noticed, and I certainly noticed others who smoked with a certain flair. Delusions die hard. What I chose to ignore then and for many years after was that smoking causes stained teeth, smelly breath, burns in favorite shirts or sweaters, and clothes that smell like dirty ashtrays.

Smokers, with every pull, are making emphatic statements about themselves, their attitude toward life, their level of self-respect, and their respect for those of us sharing their space. It's helpful to remember that smokers, such as we recently were, are choosing to disregard our desire to enjoy clean air. They are selfishly unconcerned with our health and well-being, along with their own. Having opted for slow suicide, they are unfortunately willing to foist a similar fate on those of us who must breathe their air. Our example as a smoker who has quit is the most powerful statement we can make.

**I will have opportunities today to set an example for someone
else who really would like to quit. The decision to do so needs
my support.**

Stop Smoking and Vaping Now!

Day 26

"I had to take quitting little by little."

Making the decision to stop using tobacco is the first step, and that is a step we've taken. But there are many additional steps in the process of quitting; we can only go forward one day at a time, one step at a time.

It's helpful if we renew our commitment to quitting every morning. It's also helpful if we turn within ourselves for the strength to move through the urges that will assuredly arise throughout the day, particularly at those times when, in the past, we eagerly relied on a cigarette to calm our nerves or to distract us from a painful moment.

We all know someone who did smoke but who doesn't anymore. Giving someone the opportunity to help us through these early weeks will strengthen each of us. It's a rare person who simply lays aside nicotine and goes forward with no regrets.

Let me feel no shame for my struggle today. It's a mighty and worthy endeavor to choose a life free from tobacco.

Day 27

---

*"I soon learned that no urge ever lasts more
than thirty seconds."*

Urges to smoke are so powerful. They momentarily obsess us, and we feel crazy with desire. It's helpful to know that urges are normal and fleeting. All we need to do is let them go. They will run their course in a matter of moments, and our attention will be captured by another thought or a fresh situation.

Urges serve as strong reminders of the power of nicotine, but urges can be accepted as gifts that support our decision not to smoke. Our lives as smokers weren't our own. Tobacco was in control of our thoughts, our attitudes, and our behavior. Perhaps we'd forget the insidious control nicotine exerts if it weren't for the reminders the urges offer us.

**When an urge tempts me today, I'll be grateful for the
reminder that nicotine does not easily give up its prey.**

Day 28

---

*"Smoking is poison for my body. I need my body
to live. I owe myself that respect."*

I liked smoking. It felt like my friend and it comforted me, I thought. Only now do I realize smoking was an enemy in disguise—an enemy to my body, to the bodies of others subjected to my smoking, and to the environment housing us all.

It's helpful imaging tobacco with a skull and crossbones. In these early days of quitting, we need constant reminders of the dangers inherent in smoking, to our lungs and hearts and to the lungs and hearts of other people—whether they are friends, coworkers, or strangers. We are human bodies sharing this planet, and each of us has a responsibility for the preservation of all of us.

**My physical body needs my loving attention, my care, and
gentle nurturing in order for it to serve me fully today
and in my many days ahead.**

Day 29

"The best part of not smoking is the freedom."

Cigarettes tied me down. Thinking, talking, daydreaming, reading, driving—they all sought cigarettes as accompaniment. Some of us thought we wouldn't be able to do any of these things alone, without the companionship of a cigarette. Some days it's very hard to "go it alone."

And yet, we've got a few days of freedom from nicotine. How good it feels to know that tobacco is no longer more powerful than we are. Today I will keep track of all the activities I'm enjoying without a cigarette, a nicotine vape, or a pinch of tobacco.

How glad I am that I can sit here quietly reading this meditation and not be in need of a cigarette.

Day 30

---

*"I had been putting off quitting for years.
But now I've done it!"*

There's generally a lot of planning and talk, along with a few false starts, before we are able to leave cigarettes alone. And that's all part of the process. There is no right way to quit. There are as many ways to quit as there are smokers who want to give up tobacco.

Self-talk to support the decision to quit is valuable because our subconscious tucks away all the information we feed it. Affirming we are happy nonsmokers, particularly on every occasion when we'd normally have smoked a cigarette or two, will help to break the old pattern of behavior while at the same time creating a new image of ourselves. We have tremendous power as individuals to determine who we want to be and to strengthen those traits that will foster the identity that best suits us.

**I am happy not smoking. I savor the strength I feel from
sticking to this decision.**

Day 31

---

*"If it's possible to stop smoking for an hour,
it's possible to stop smoking for good."*

This moment is all we have. It's all we'll ever have. Our yesterdays are gone; regardless of what they held for us, they are past, and we survived them. All we can ever be sure of experiencing for the remainder of this life is what we are involved with right now. And right now, whether we're in turmoil or euphoria, we don't need a cigarette to survive.

The future is unknown and illusory. Moment by moment, the future becomes our present and introduces us to exactly what we need to grow. We've been promised the strength to move through our particular moments, and cigarettes can neither hasten nor help us with the steps we'll need to take.

It's helpful to take an inventory of the various experiences we've had since quitting tobacco. Many of them were stressful; and yet we're still here now, and we didn't need to smoke to get here. We've had fearful periods, too, and we didn't smoke. We're learning, day by day, that no experience is too much for us to handle without a cigarette, and every experience is offering us information to grow.

**I've learned it is possible to stop smoking for an hour.
Fortunately, our lives are just a very long collection of hours.**

Stop Smoking and Vaping Now!

Day 32

"Nonsmoking living is so day-to-day. It sometimes takes a minute-to-minute kind of new identity."

It's harder not to smoke some days. A frustrating encounter with a coworker or an emotionally charged argument with a friend or lover can make us hunger for a cigarette. Cigarettes used to comfort us. Feeling our anger or hurt or fear is oftentimes painful and very draining. Sometimes we miss the quiet comfort and freedom that smoking gave us. Smoking seemed like a friend then.

If smoking tempts me today, I'll remember my growth as a person depends on knowing and feeling whatever feelings are triggered by the day's events. And I'll remember smoking was never really a friend. Rather, smoking stunted my growth; it took away my power to make healthy choices.

**When the urge to escape from today's lessons comes,
I'll be quietly thankful that in a saner moment
I chose to quit nicotine.**

Day 33

"I literally looked myself in the mirror more than once and said, 'You are a nonsmoker, and you want to stay that way.'"

We need to employ many techniques to stay committed to our decision not to smoke. Tobacco, like alcohol, is cunning, baffling, and powerful. The desire to smoke "just one" won't be a rare desire. And if we've let down our guard against starting again, if we've gotten complacent about the strength of the addiction, then we are very vulnerable to the appeal of "just one."

We must ask for the support of other nonsmokers throughout our early recovery from smoking. We must be willing to live through frequent urges to smoke and accept our powerlessness over those urges. More importantly, we must be willing to take responsibility for who we are and who we want to be. Standing before a mirror and reminding ourselves of who we are is a powerful tool in this struggle for growth.

When the urge to smoke strikes, I can either be my own best friend or my own worst enemy.

Day 34

"I'm a committed nonsmoker, and I love it part of the time; but not always. I really do see quitting as a process."

Most of us can't just quit one day and never touch tobacco again. We stop and start and stop and start. And hopefully, we'll one day stop forever. Even when that day comes, however, we may not be contented nonsmokers. Some days the idea of a cigarette is appealing. Hopefully, we'll be able to remember that one cigarette will never be enough.

To not want to smoke and yet to love the thought of one cigarette is familiar thinking during these early weeks of tobacco-free living. Let's not be concerned with our confusion nor even with our strong desire to smoke. Desire can't make us act against our will. It can only tempt and tease us. The decision to smoke is separate from the desire.

I'll seek support from friends if I'm wavering in my decision-making ability today.

Day 35

"I quit every day and then smoked every day, too."

The desire to smoke is so overpowering some days. Every activity, every memory, every anticipated event seems to beg for a cigarette. But with the help of friends who want us to be able to quit, and the help of our inner spirit, who really does wish us good health and freedom from this addiction, we can move beyond the momentary cravings that crowd us throughout the course of the day.

We need not repeat past patterns where we quit and then smoke again all too quickly. This time can be different if we are prepared to respond differently to the urges to smoke.

**I look forward to living through an urge today with the help
of friends, both internally and externally.**

Day 36

"After I first quit, I would begin a project or begin reading or doing something with my hands, but I couldn't stay at it for long."

Did cigarettes foster concentration within us? It's doubtful, but it may seem that way now as we're struggling with our preoccupation with nicotine. It's no wonder that we can't complete our work. Our attention span is so sporadic. But our thoughts don't happen to us; we are in charge of them, and our obsessive thinking about tobacco is directly attributable to ourselves, which means we can have the power to change the program whenever we desire. Fortunate indeed!

The realization that we are in command of our thoughts as well as our feelings is a powerful one. But it might also terrify us because it lays at our feet full responsibility for whatever we dwell on, whatever we see in others, and whatever we feel in response to any experience that has our attention. There can be no more blaming others for our own feelings or actions.

I'm in charge of my own movie reel today. I can enjoy the day fully if I so choose.

Day 37

"I know what this addiction is; and I know if I smoke even one cigarette, I may not be able to give up smoking again."

Wavering from our commitment to stop, even for just one quick puff, is a choice we'd best not make. One cigarette looks so innocent; but for an addict, there is no such thing as only one. Giving in to the urge allows the addiction to take control. Most of us have had experience with our own loss of control myriad times before. Let's not forget our earlier failed attempts to quit; even more important, let's remember the many avenues of help available to us if we seek them.

Almost anybody is willing to listen for a moment if we're struggling with an urge today. And that will strengthen us. If we're feeling lonely and caught in fond recall of the comfort cigarettes seemed to offer, now is our opportunity to let a friend step into the void with us, thus making two people feel worthy and comforted.

It's possible to think of urges to smoke as gifts honoring our growth, proving we let the urge guide us toward others or to a Higher Power for strength. Isolating ourselves with an urge gives the urge undeserved power.

Some days will be easier than others without cigarettes. The tough days will bring us closer to others, and that's something to be grateful for.

Day 38

"Since I've quit smoking, I'm no longer destroying my clothes and my furniture on a regular basis."

Smoking is such a dirty and dangerous habit. We'll never know how many children, women, men, and others have died as the result of someone's smoking. Houses burn down; cars are wrecked; lungs are destroyed. What a relief to no longer be contributing to the destruction cigarettes cause.

Those of us struggling to be nonsmokers need each other's support, along with the support of our friends and family. Giving up our steady companion results in feelings of loneliness. It's time to strengthen our companionship with others who, like us, don't smoke. In the process, we will be setting a good example for someone else who may also want to try life as a nonsmoker.

I will remember I'm setting a positive example for someone else today.

Day 39

"I realized I had gone through half a day without a cigarette, and I hadn't come apart at the seams; so I decided to keep going with it."

Quitting seemed tentative initially. It was more of a hope than commitment for most of us. And what a surprise we had when we survived that first day—and then the first week. Self-esteem began to build. "I can do it!" But we still hesitated to announce it too loudly—just in case.

Now, it's a few weeks later. Sometimes we feel like we're barely hanging on. The urges to smoke still come, and we wonder why. The fond recall of smoking frequently overwhelms us; at times like those, let's not hesitate to ask for help from our friends.

Quitting a habit that has befriended us for years is very difficult. We truly can't comfortably do it alone. And that's okay. In fact, that's good. We all need to nurture our reliance on others for help. We weren't meant to live our lives in solitary confinement. Our resources for strength exist outside ourselves—in our friends—as well as within.

Any day that I'm struggling, I pray I can remember to turn to my network of friends. We are in this life to help one another.

Day 40

"I no longer wake up in the middle of the night and have to smoke a cigarette before I can get back to sleep."

Sleeping straight through a night has been one of the unexpected, pleasurable results of life without tobacco. In the early weeks of our recovery from tobacco use, we likely slept much more than usual. For many of us accustomed to waking in the night, perhaps we never connected sleepless spells with nicotine deprivation. But our bodies were attuned to the many hours without tobacco. More restful sleeping is just one of the many benefits now gracing our nights and the days that follow.

What a miracle it is to be living through every moment of every day without cigarettes. We're not free of the desire, perhaps; nor are we always content with our decision to quit. It's normal for us to grieve the loss, and even feel occasional anger over the choice we've made to not smoke. Fortunately, we don't have to shoulder any of our feelings alone. We have other nonsmokers to turn to for support and understanding, and we have the strength of a Higher Power who is always available to us.

I'll remember the miracle of my freedom from tobacco all day long.

Day 41

*"When I finally got through my withdrawal,
I tapped into the faith that I really would come out
on the other side."*

There is no doubt that we will "come out on the other side." We will survive the arduous process of stopping smoking, even though some of our days have been very difficult and we've wanted so badly to smoke again. What a tantalizing thought to have "just one." But we must not forget that for us, there's no such thing as "just one."

When this struggle feels overwhelming, let's remember we're not alone. On this very day, there are no doubt thousands, and perhaps tens of thousands, who likewise are choosing to become nonsmokers. Imagining a group of us cheering each other on will lessen our pain and lighten our dark moods.

Our attitude is awesomely powerful. We can use it to our advantage each time conditions tempt us to renege on our commitment to not smoke.

**What a marvelous image a cheering group of nonsmokers
makes. I'll visualize us many times today.**

Day 42

_____

"I suddenly realized I had actual control
over how I felt."

It's a strengthening awareness to know that we, and we alone, are responsible for how we feel. For years perhaps, we've wanted to blame others. "He makes me so mad!" "She did it to me again!" Ultimately, we have to accept full responsibility for how we feel. Even the direst conditions can't get us down without our consent. We are willingly, though maybe unconsciously, opting for the anger, the depression, or the feelings of inadequacy that are troubling us today.

Without tobacco to muffle our feelings, we're much more aware of how frequently we entertain destructive feelings. They chart our course of action; and most often, it's a course that a more thoughtful and peaceful mind wouldn't have taken.

We can and should take conscious, careful control of our moods, our thoughts, and our actions. Never are we puppets whose strings are being manipulated by foes or friends. We are actors in control of ourselves throughout every scene of this play called life.

_____

I will consciously choose my feelings today.
No one is in charge but me!

_____

Day 43

"There's absolutely no question smoking damages one's health."

When the urge to smoke arises today, as it most likely will, it's helpful to remind ourselves that smoking kills men, women, and children. Not only will we be at risk for cancer, heart disease, and home fires if we smoke, we'll put those we care about most at risk, too. To not smoke is a decision, and one that we might need to make over and over today as urges beckon.

Most of us have known one person who has experienced surgery or at least hospitalization because of the effects of tobacco. We've all heard a horror story about the agonizing death of a cancer patient, but we've generally tended to believe it couldn't happen to us. Choosing a smoke-free life won't guarantee our absolute safety, but not smoking is a pretty good insurance policy. Smoking does damage health—ours and our children's.

I'll be grateful for the gift I'm giving myself and my family today by not smoking.

Day 44

"My experience taught me that if you really want to quit, just keep trying."

It's disheartening to quit smoking and then begin again. We feel ashamed and angry, and maybe even depressed that we couldn't remain committed to our resolve. And somewhat embarrassingly, we probably even feel a little relief that the struggle to not smoke is over, at least for a while.

Those of us reading these words are lucky. We have made the decision once again to live a day at a time without cigarettes. And this time can be different. We can rely on support from friends and other nonsmokers—people who genuinely want to help us. Each time an urge to smoke overcomes us, we can read this meditation again and again throughout the day. We have permission to go to any lengths to not smoke—if that's our choice.

We can be just as successful with not smoking as we can be playing a clarinet, a game of tennis, or a game of cards. Practice is the key—practice and the willingness to experience the struggle.

**Today I'll remember the old adage that
"practice makes perfect."**

Day 45

"Cigarettes were my companion, my solace."

Giving up anything we love—pie, chocolate, liquor, or cigarettes—makes us feel deprived. So it's not surprising we feel abandoned without our cigarettes to comfort us. But we have the choice to see our deprivation as an opportunity to seek solace from the people in our lives—men and women who are not simply surrounding us by chance. They've been handpicked by our Higher Power and theirs. Together, we have miles to go and much to learn.

This design for our lives is mysterious, but it is loving and promises us growth. We can trust that we'll not be led astray; rather, we'll be introduced to all the experiences meant for our fuller development. Meeting these experiences without the false aid of cigarettes promises a clearer understanding of their meaning.

Let's not deprive ourselves of all the beauty, knowledge, and growth meant for us by giving undue attention to the fleeting moments of deprivation we feel over the loss of tobacco.

**I'll look lovingly upon my network of friends today
and recognize they are not here by chance.**

Day 46

"Quitting cold turkey means changing your whole attitude, and it will never happen overnight."

Patience is indeed a virtue, one seldom possessed by people like us who still yearn for the mysterious contentment offered by a cigarette. We wanted to quit painlessly and to go on with our lives unchanged. But everything has changed, and the unfamiliarity of our surfacing feelings brings little pleasure as we've defined it. The power and the choice to redefine it rests with us.

It's a time to be gentle with ourselves and to reflect on the distance we've traveled since childhood, trusting we'll move through this period of discontent with as much comfort as we decide to muster. Quitting smoking was a major decision and an even more demanding undertaking. Let's be patient and tolerant of our inner upheaval. Time will heal.

**I'll remind myself that patience will reward me tenfold today.
I'll realize the benefits in all my tomorrows.**

Day 47

"One of the pluses of not smoking is I can play good racquetball. All of a sudden I feel I can play forever again."

No more breathlessness from climbing a short flight of stairs—even running to catch a bus is a possibility now. No longer are we embarrassed by incessant coughing that we as well as our friends and coworkers knew was from our smoking. In a matter of weeks, we can see the evidence of healthy physical changes. And the improvements have just begun.

It's human nature to discount these improvements in our physical condition. We quickly forget we always used to opt for an elevator rather than taking the stairs. But our bodies will continue to renew themselves even without our attention. we are more aware of our mental condition; our self-esteem is on an upswing. We're proud and grateful we've taken back our power from nicotine. We can share our gratitude by helping someone else who wants to stop.

I didn't get free of my addiction alone. I'll be available to support someone who wants to follow my example today.

Day 48

---

*"Smoking is really an out-and-out statement that
'I don't care about myself.'
I'm glad I'm not saying that anymore."*

Smoking was glamorous or sexy, we thought. This might have been the attraction when we took that first puff. How different our perception is now. We have changed, and our growth is significant. As smokers, there was little we could do—whether reading, conversing, driving, or simply kicking back—without a cigarette as a crutch. Now we know the laughter and good times, the quiet, romantic moments, and the problem-solving situations are even more rewarding when we're not encumbered by tobacco and its necessary paraphernalia.

Change and growth, like spring and flowers, are paired. And it's good for us to meditate on our positive changes. As humans, we need to feel glory in our growth and experience an awareness that we are moving forward. Our quiet reflection will strengthen our decision and our connection to the inner power that has comforted us throughout the struggle.

**I'll take some time today to sit quietly and dwell on
who I'm becoming, and I'll be grateful for the growth.**

Day 49

"Smoking makes connecting with people difficult."

We've no doubt come to realize what an intrusion smoking was in our lives. We're particularly aware of this when we're in the company of others who smoke. Their attention to the conversation is frequently fleeting. The search for the elusive book of matches or lighter never fails to take precedence.

We do well to remember what it was like for us as smokers. Let's not forget the frantic searches for cigarettes at two in the morning, the concern over our lack of wind on a tennis court, or the dread of going without nicotine in no-smoking meetings or in homes bearing the sign, "Thank you for not smoking or vaping."

Smoking, like any addiction, can become more important than even the dearest friend. It does ruin lives and relationships, and it sets a poor example for young minds that are so eager to imitate. Isn't it well to have nicotine dependency be a thing of our past?

I'll pay special attention to all the times others' cigarettes intrude on my space today, and I'll be glad I've found freedom.

Day 50

---

*"One of the positive things that happened right away
after quitting was the release from fear."*

The harmful effects of nicotine, whether smoked or vaped, have made the news very frequently over the last few years. We've been educated about the danger it poses to our lungs, heart, and circulatory system. Famous people who've died from the ravages of cancer have made the nightly news. The less fortunate among us have been more personally affected. Perhaps a friend or relative died. Even worse, some of us sharing this present struggle are recovering from cancer surgery.

Having quit gives each of us an extended lease on life, giving us a multidimensional gift of freedom. It frees us from the fear that we'll die an awful cancer-ridden death. Quitting gives us freedom from an addiction that demanded our time, our money, and our attention, and releases us from the embarrassment we felt when we couldn't spend time in someone's car, or an evening in someone's home or in a favorite restaurant, without a nicotine fix at frequent intervals.

**I'll reflect on my freedom today and be grateful
that I have taken charge of my life.**

Day 51

---

*"I still think of tobacco every day even though
I'm happier not using it."*

Tobacco acted as our friend, accompanying us everywhere we went. It shouldn't surprise us that we think of our 'friend' perhaps many times throughout a day. When a close friend moves away, we think of her or him often, wishing we could share a triumph or a saddening experience. But we don't have to reach for a phone. We can go to another friend for support or laughter. Likewise, we don't have to reach for a cigarette. We can let the thought slip away and turn our attention to the present.

We're happier not using tobacco because we know we made a wise and healthy decision, and we're empowered by it. Our spirits are strengthened, having quit an activity that oftentimes embarrassed us, frequently impaired our health, and cost us a great deal in money and in peace of mind. We may waver at times and momentarily wish for a cigarette—and that's okay. It's impossible to be happy at every moment doing what's in our best interest, but making better choices yields long-term rewards.

**When I think of tobacco today, I'll say a small prayer
of gratitude for my decision to not use.**

Stop Smoking and Vaping Now!

Day 52

"My self-talk saved me."

We are not victims of the thoughts that crowd our minds. We are in charge of our thoughts, and we can change their content at will—a fact that surprises all too many people. It's familiar to feel powerless over changing our lives, and it's deadly to sidestep our responsibility.

We're the only ones who can change the course of our lives through changing our thoughts. Reprogramming our minds is a simple process. When we replace a negative judgment or an unwanted desire with a quiet mind, a positive feeling or thought will surface—every time. We may have to repeat the process many times over, but that's okay. Negative thinking was repetitive too.

We can replace the urge to smoke with a quiet mind and gladness that we're able to let the urges pass. In time, this process will be familiar, natural, and spirit-moving.

I am the master of my thoughts. I'll insist on peaceful, helpful ones today.

Day 53

---

*"No longer killing myself on an installment plan
feels wonderful."*

When we quit smoking, we also quit deluding ourselves about the harm nicotine does to the body. It kills, and our lungs have been damaged. Time is a healer.

Even though we've been off cigarettes only a few weeks, a glance in the mirror reveals cleaner teeth and clearer skin. Our pores are no longer clogged with the toxins from nicotine. Even our hair is shinier and less brittle. Nicotine squeezed life from every part of our body. Time is healing us.

All we've had to do is stop smoking, and every part of our physical body is beginning to adjust to this freedom from the killing effects of nicotine. But sometimes we have to personally intervene to help our attitude to adjust. It is not every day that we are content without the numbing effects of nicotine. Some days we fail to appreciate having more energy, cleaner teeth, and healthier skin. Let's look for support from others who understand our struggle on the rough days. Tough times will come—but they will go.

I'm in charge of my attitude. A moment of silence will help me adjust it.

Stop Smoking *and Vaping* Now!

Day 54

"Quitting was not physically difficult, but quitting any activity that rewards you means losing something from your life."

Grieving is a natural and healthy response when we've experienced a loss, particularly the loss of someone or something that has been dear to us over a long period. Tobacco is such a thing. For all the years we smoked, we were seldom, if ever, more than an arm's reach from a cigarette; we were probably closer to a cigarette than we'd even been to a very close friend. We used cigarettes for comfort, to keep us awake, to soothe anxieties, and to signify a breather from a difficult or tedious task. Our excuses for why we should smoke undoubtedly ran into the hundreds.

Giving up cigarettes means we're confronted with hours of activities that have to be handled unaided each day. Of course, we're managing this, and we've been off tobacco for a few weeks now; but the grieving process most likely is yet to be completed. Let's not be concerned. Let's rejoice that we are surviving the loss. Let's rest assured that the grief will pass and that our satisfaction with being a nonsmoker will escalate. Time is all we need.

Each of these twenty-four hours ahead of me today will help the grief die and heighten my happiness with being a nonsmoker.

Day 55

"When I was involved in a self-indulgent, pleasure-oriented activity like smoking, I was effectively tuned out from the rest of the world."

Very often, conversations failed to keep our attention, and activities like running or tennis were much too demanding of our energy when our focus was on our primary relationship with tobacco. For all the years we've smoked, tobacco was *the* primary relationship in our lives. Sure, we had friends and family whom we loved; but when the body cried out for nicotine, we responded regardless of what others needed from us at the moment.

We don't look at our smoking past with a great deal of pride. What we can feel good about is that it is now part of the past. We have charted a new course for ourselves, one that's much healthier and more respectful toward ourselves and our loved ones. No longer does smoking distract us from circumstances and individuals who are in our lives by design. We're free now to more attentively fill our role in their lives.

**I'm free today to be fully present to all the people
and experiences in my life.**

Day 56

"Prior to quitting, if I was upset about something,
I would smoke rather than deal with it."

As smokers, we all had so many repressed emotions, and they ate at us, causing both stress and anxiety that clouded most of our waking moments. Because of our smoking, we were unconsciously dishonest with ourselves and with our families and friends. Our feelings were not genuinely felt and shared, which fostered our dishonesty with the people who loved us the most. Relationships are only as strong and healthy as they are open and honest.

As nonsmokers, we can look forward to new beginnings with the important people in our lives. The past is gone. We need not lament the shortcomings that plagued us in that earlier time. The future offers all we need for personal growth, for inner happiness, and for our sense of belonging with the people who surround us. Our future as nonsmokers will be far different from what would have been in store for us had we not so wisely chosen this new path.

This new path I walk today offers me chances I had never dared hope for in years past.

Day 57

"My baby will grow up with a role model
who doesn't smoke."

We have all learned from observing others in our lives. Often, we painstakingly imitated the behavior and the gestures of people we admired. Our heroes weren't always exemplary role models. Nevertheless, their influence was strong; as our characters developed, we created ourselves in their likeness. How awesome it is to be reminded that we, too, are role models. Others, young and old, may look to us today for the strength to make changes in their lives. Living a smoke-free lifestyle is a refreshing statement to be making to onlookers. We've needed others to help us make this commitment day after smoke-free day. Perhaps it's our turn now to willingly lend our support and share our strength and hope with someone else.

I'll not forget my responsibility to set a good example today.
I may be helping someone when I least expect it.

Stop Smoking and Vaping Now!

Day 58

"I had a million incidences of quitting for two weeks,
quitting for three months, quitting for twenty minutes."

Tobacco is a drug, one that we easily got hooked by. To get unhooked takes first a willingness, then a decision, and finally a commitment to experience the pain-filled moments without giving in to the urge to smoke again.

Anytime we've quit and started again, it's only because we gave in to the urge. The urges will always come. But we have the choice to call a friend for support, to help reaffirm our decision not to smoke and to recount the benefits gained from not smoking. In the past, we gave in because the urge was stronger than our decision. It was also stronger than our self-love.

This can be the last time I need to quit if that's what I want.
The choice is mine alone.

Day 59

---

*"Talking to former smokers and asking them to listen
is wonderful support during the hard times."*

It is not easy becoming a nonsmoker, particularly a contented one. Some days, some experiences, some ordinary moments will test our resolve to the limit. At times like these, we need the strength and support of others who have survived this process before us.

And it will help to remember our decision to quit was not a hasty one. We want to be free of tobacco. We don't want to let a thirty-second urge take away our freedom and our will.

**I can call upon friends who understand the intensity of my
urge to use tobacco. A sympathetic ear will take away the
loneliness of my struggle today.**

Stop Smoking and Vaping Now!

Day 60

"The best thing about not smoking is it doesn't have
any power over me anymore."

Today might be a good day to remember how tied we were to cigarettes, pipes, chewing tobacco, or vaping. We should not quickly forget how insanely we protected our supply—smoking dead butts in the early morning hours or driving in a blinding storm to the nearest store or gas station because, infuriatingly, we had run out.

How nice it is to get out of bed free of any need to search for a lighter or vape pen. And what fun it is to be free of needing to fill a pocket or purse with our supplies. Newspapers, coffee, and phone conversations are just as stimulating without nicotine. Thankfully, we've taken back power over our lives.

I'll gratefully relish my freedom today, and I'll appreciate
the blessings of being a nonsmoker.

Day 61

"I struggled, quitting all alone."

Quitting smoking or vaping is still a daily decision for many of us. And it's a decision we must make for ourselves. We've probably tried to quit countless times before—for a spouse, a parent, or our children—and failed in our attempts. We want this attempt to be successful. It's a lonely and individual decision, but we don't have to cope with the struggle to live with our decision alone. And for that we can be grateful.

To be sure, quitting smoking is a difficult experience, and it's always our choice to struggle through any difficult experience alone if we prefer. But we have other options. We can look to our inner strength, which offers us a partnership strong enough to handle even the most trying circumstance without the aid of a cigarette. And we can look to friends or others around us who, like us, are developing a new pattern of living, one that doesn't include dependence on nicotine.

Day 62

"When I see other people smoke,
I'm glad it's not me."

I'm well on my way to becoming a comfortable nonsmoker. I no longer connect smoking with all my routine activities. I've become accustomed to finishing a meal without a cigarette. The beverages I drink can be enjoyed without cigarettes. Neither a drive across town nor reading a newspaper require the companionship of a cigarette. I feel good and strengthened by the choices I've made.

Throughout this day, I'll be mindful of all the times in the past when I would have lit a cigarette. I am not compelled to do it any longer; and I'll willingly share my story with someone else who'd like to travel this road, too.

Day 63

"I really don't want to smoke again.
And I think I'm free."

When we know we really don't want to smoke again, the biggest part of our struggle is over. In the past, we may have quit to satisfy someone else or perhaps because we knew smoking was detrimental to our health. When we quit for any reason other than that we no longer want to smoke, the struggle with the impulse to smoke again looms large in our experience. It's important to reflect on how far we've come.

I feel free from my smoking past today, and it's good to tally up the advantages of not smoking. My health is improving. I have more energy and better lung capacity. My living space is cleaner at home, at work, and in my car, and this benefits me and all who share these spaces. I have more money. I'm no longer self-conscious about finding a place to smoke in public. Best of all, taking back my power rather than letting nicotine dependency continue to rule my life has enhanced my self-worth a hundredfold.

I really don't want to smoke again, and I know I'm free today.

Stop Smoking and Vaping Now!

Day 64

"I decided early on I wasn't going to let the weight gain bother me too much because I think it will adjust itself over time."

First things first: Not smoking is the priority. Yet it's terribly frustrating to struggle with extra pounds when we're trying so hard to make a major improvement in our lives. We've come to know that gaining weight is a common dilemma for most of us who have chosen this new direction. And dealing with it will one day be our top priority. But for today, once again, not smoking is the number one priority.

I've become accustomed to conversations without cigarettes, to car trips with both hands on the wheel, to sipping coffee and reading the news free from the distraction of billowing smoke or vapor. There was a time when most activities were difficult to live through without nicotine as a crutch. But live I did.

How happy I am that I took the suggestion of "First Things First."

Day 65

"Smoking is very much a barrier between people."

Smoking was a very distracting activity. There was the constant reaching for a cigarette, the unending search for a lighter or matches, and the necessary dumping of dirty, overflowing ashtrays. All of these activities usually occurred in the midst of an important visit with a friend or an urgent phone call. We simply couldn't give full attention to the friend. Our eyes and hands would always dart here or there looking for the paraphernalia we desperately needed.

And then there was the smoke—clouds of it billowing between our faces, preventing an open, clear view of each other's faces. How hard it is to divulge our inner selves when we can't see our friend's eyes.

Finally, there are the muffled feelings smoking causes, which means we're not being 100 percent real with the people who love us.

**How grateful I am that I've removed the barrier
between my loved ones and myself.**

Day 66

"When I realized I could not quit smoking, that I was so addicted it was out of my control and I could not quit, then I was able to stop."

Each of us has had a unique experience with nicotine, how we've used it, and how we got free of it, or struggled to get free. And for none of us has this new identity as a nonsmoker come with total ease. Some of us tricked ourselves into it. Or maybe we bargained with ourselves. Quitting for a spell and then rewarding ourselves with a smoke is common, too.

There is real wisdom in finally admitting our powerlessness over addiction. When we can do that, we discover a freedom from the compulsion to smoke, and, mysteriously, the personal power to stop using and stay stopped.

We can and will become contented nonsmokers. Each day we will experience a greater level of freedom from the compulsion to smoke.

Today I will be grateful for stopping smoking.

Day 67

"I had gone through so much in my life to be a healthy, strong woman; and I didn't want to kill myself with cigarettes."

For many of us, quitting smoking or vaping feels like the most difficult thing we've ever survived; and that's a natural reaction. Nicotine is addictive, and the body learned to expect the frequent jolts nicotine provided.

The more years we inhaled smoke or vapor, the more difficult it is to retrain the body's expectations. But it can be done; we are doing it. Every time we release an urge to smoke without acting on that impulse, we are supporting a new, much healthier behavior.

In the midst of a craving for nicotine (and cravings will likely haunt us for weeks), we'd do well to remember the many other challenges we've survived. From these we will gain strength. And we lived through every single one of those challenges: divorce, the death of a loved one, job loss, separation from family and friends. We've survived—even though we often felt unsure we could. We'll survive this struggle, too. That's the process of human life. Becoming a comfortable nonsmoker is just the next step for all of us reading these words.

I'll try to remember today I'm not alone in my struggle to be a nonsmoker. There are many of us, right now, sharing these same words.

Stop Smoking *and* Vaping Now!

Day 68

---

*"What I learned was that to become a happy
nonsmoker, it helped to think of myself as one."*

Our thoughts determine who we are and who we will become. Their power over us, particularly how we feel about ourselves, is awesome. It's very important to remember our thoughts are not given to us by an external source. They are very much our own, created solely by ourselves, which means each of us has the personal power along with the responsibility to decide what thoughts we want to entertain. No thought has the power to dominate our focus without our giving in to it.

Knowing we are responsible for our own thoughts can be both frightening and hopeful—frightening because it forces the issue of taking responsibility, but hopeful because we can choose to be as happy as we make up our minds to be. It is strengthening to understand and accept responsibility for moving our lives in a new, more positive direction. "Life" doesn't simply happen to us. We are cocreators every step of the way.

**Every thought I have today is of my own making. I will create
strengthening, faith-filled thoughts that will protect me
throughout the day.**

Day 69

---

*"I can remember walking down the street the first spring
after quitting and smelling lilacs before I saw them.
That was powerful."*

Taking careful note, and perhaps even making a list of the positive changes in our physical condition, our attitudes, and our perceptions since quitting smoking or vaping can offer important reinforcement for this decision we have made. The pull to smoke again will happen; as a safety measure to protect us from the urge, we can refer to our list of positive changes.

We need to be grateful for the increased energy we have; the improved self-image; the absence of embarrassment from being singled out in restaurants; and the regained ability to smell and taste the myriad treats offered throughout a day. It will never be wasted energy to count our newfound blessings as nonsmokers. These blessings are real and earned through hard work and commitment. And these blessings will continue to multiply as do the days of living free of nicotine.

**I'll begin my day by counting my blessings,
and I'll look for a new one, too.**

Day 70

"Smokers are in prison."

Nicotine used to be in control of our lives. It helped us wake up, we thought. It brought us peace and confidence when we were riddled with anxiety. It smoothed our conversations with strangers. Tobacco was king—it was our god in all matters concerning us. We were at its mercy, bowing to its demands—rifling our pockets and wastebaskets for a lonely cigarette or a smokeable butt, or driving miles in a blinding storm rather than live through the night without the security of a smoke.

The degradation to which we stooped may haunt us. And it's right that we recall those times. Never should we forget the power nicotine wields. We should always remember we're only a puff away from giving tobacco the upper hand once again.

The choice to quit smoking was the right one for us. Let's not ever let the reality of our lives as smokers be clouded by a momentary euphoric recall.

Smoking made me a prisoner in my own home, and car, and skin. My sentence is over!

Day 71

"I realize now I always smelled like smoke."

Few of us realized how offensive the odors clinging to us were. Our clothes, hair, and breath quickly labeled us as smokers. Our homes and automobiles were seldom pleasant environments for nonsmokers. It was as though we were immersed in an impenetrable and offensive cloud that settled wherever we settled. Not a pretty image. Not a favorite recollection.

It's exhilarating and refreshing to smell clean. The stains on our teeth and fingers have disappeared. We can detect the scents of spring, summer, fall, and winter wafting through the air. And we can identify a smoker very quickly.

Let's be grateful we're no longer polluting our own air, or someone else's.

I'll breathe deeply today and appreciate my own improved smells, along with the aromas of Mother Nature.

Day 72

---

*"My process for stopping began
with a decision to stop."*

Building a house, writing a book, or even just taking a course in taxation can be overwhelming if we limit our focus to the end result rather than doing what we need to do one day at a time to get it done. It's the same with becoming a comfortable nonsmoker.

We had to first make the decision to stop smoking. How we will feel on a certain day may not be how we felt the day we quit; even now, in our third month, we still struggle. In time, the urges to smoke will leave altogether and the memories associated with smoking will no longer be fond recollections.

The early process is tedious, sometimes stirring both anger and depression because we don't want to be obsessed with cigarettes anymore, but we too often are. Being patient with ourselves and others when we're thinking about cigarettes rather than work or play takes extraordinary effort. It's well to remember that no thought forms in our minds without our willing participation. We're in charge. Just by deciding to do so, we can replace any thought with another thought far more to our benefit.

**My process is slow; just these twenty-four hours should
concern me, and I can do anything for one day.**

Day 73

---

*"I've come to know that smoking
is a screen between people."*

Smoking took our attention, taking the place of other parts of life to which we might have given our focus. It was all too easy to divert our emotional energy from the human beings laying claim to our presence when we were intent on vaping or smoking a cigarette.

Smoke, curling up from our ashtray, blocked our view of another person. The smoke was a subtle yet persistent physical barrier between two hearts needing to connect.

It's never by chance that we're drawn toward one another; and when we're shielding ourselves with a cloud of smoke, we're interfering with the full measure of growth that's in store for us. Let us look at each other with unclouded sight.

**There's nothing preventing me from being fully attentive
to my loved ones today.**

Day 74

---

*"I've noticed since I quit smoking
I have much more energy."*

Not all of us care about extra energy for racquetball or touch football, but it's nice and extremely noticeable that we can handle a staircase with greater ease. We can stroll while conversing with a friend without getting breathless. Our lungs will return to an earlier state of healthiness. This one decision has guaranteed us much more than greater energy; it promises a fuller, longer life.

We've no doubt noticed many changes since giving up cigarettes. The days seem to have more hours. Our clothes stay cleaner. There's a sheen to our hair that had not been there for many years. Food is no longer bland, and the windows in our cars and homes are free of the yellowish tobacco film that coated them. The changes wrought by our decision to quit smoking are far-reaching. It was a good decision, one whose impact is not yet fully felt. The weeks and months ahead promise additional surprises.

**I'll be grateful for my decision to live longer.
I'll anticipate the future with excitement.**

Day 75

"The main benefit for me is I expect to see
my kids grow up."

It's been demonstrated in too many lives that cigarettes are harmful and often deadly not only to the smoker, but to those who breathe the smoker's air. We're not the only beneficiaries of our decision to quit smoking; friends, children, spouses, and coworkers have been given the gift of cleaner air and the chance for longer lives.

We wonder now how we could have continued to smoke for so long. We're not dumb people, yet we ignored both statistics and our common sense. Addiction is powerful; all addictions are powerful. The only chance to comfortably find freedom from an addiction is to turn to other people, and to the spiritual presence that resides within us all, for strength and support. Let's not dwell on the past and question our sanity in regard to smoking. Let's look to the present and rejoice that "then was then and now is now."

My chances for a longer, healthier life have been vastly
improved by this one decision.

Day 76

"I sometimes miss cigarettes,
even now after all these years."

Having decided to give up cigarettes is no guarantee we won't long for an occasional smoke. It's normal for smoking memories to haunt us. Smoking was there during our celebrations and our traumas. But now, we don't need to act on a desire to smoke. Each day we experience desires we don't address—perhaps a desire to initiate a conversation with a stranger, order dessert with lunch, or call a lover for a rendezvous. Desires should be acknowledged, but there is no requirement that we give in to them.

We can't control the sun, the slow-to-bloom lilac bushes, the newspaper carrier, or the neighbor's dog. In fact, our burdens are few. Our behavior and our attitudes are all we've been assigned to control during this life span. These two assignments make us responsible for both our longing to smoke and our happiness about not smoking.

The choice is mine. Will I get on with healthy living and shake the dangerous desires away?

Day 77

"People who smoke are like people not wearing seat belts. It's passive suicide."

We were probably very content as smokers for a period of time. We liked the comfort, the familiarity, and the absence of loneliness that smoking guaranteed. How and when did this contentment change? Perhaps we can no longer recall. It's enough to remember that it did change, and we can never go back—at least not to the contentment enjoyed in former years. Now we know too much. Now we know cigarettes were slowly killing us and our loved ones. Now we know each puff drew us closer to the end of our lives.

It's startling to know and hard to accept that we were committing suicide on the installment plan. No doubt suicide was the furthest thing from our conscious minds. Yet suicide was the underlying reality, and it is the reality for millions who have yet to join our ranks.

It will bolster our own resolve to share our story—what it was like, what happened, and what it's like now—with a friend we suspect also wants to quit making installment payments.

I'll carry my story to someone today and save a life.

Day 78

"Tobacco was a friend that I now know was really an enemy."

Sometimes through unfortunate experiences, we learned that certain others in our lives were not the friends they professed to be. All too frequently, they pretended to be friends to get something from us. Cigarettes got something from us, too—our money, our peace of mind, our healthy bodies, and our souls.

As smokers, we were not acting in concert with our best interests. Cigarettes wielded great power over us, demanding our time and attention in a way not unlike an inconsiderate person. Perhaps the finest thing we can be grateful for today is that we recognized cigarettes were enemies in disguise, and we assertively took back our power.

It's not difficult to determine who is a genuine friend. Getting quiet within allows our Spirit to share the wisdom. It's that same wisdom that will guide our every act if we'll listen.

**I'll be quiet many times today and just listen within
and find direction and strength.**

Day 79

"If a person smokes a pack a day, and it takes seven minutes to smoke a cigarette, that's 140 minutes a day, almost two and a half hours spent smoking rather than doing something productive. People write books in that amount of time."

It might have seemed nearly impossible to accomplish anything in the early weeks of quitting tobacco. We were generally obsessed with smoking memories and the desire for a cigarette. But with the passage of time, we've grown accustomed to a routine that does not include the customary stops to light a cigarette.

Cigarettes *are* a thing of the past. An occasional urge may surface, but that shouldn't alarm us. Remember, we're in control of our behavior every moment, and the urges will pass.

An unexpected result of giving up cigarettes is we have additional time we can put to good use. Although we often smoked while we worked, we more often stopped working to smoke. Each of us has a list, tucked away in our minds, of things we'd like to do—perhaps take tennis lessons or a painting class, or tackle a remodeling project. Now is the time to scratch one thing off the list.

My days are longer now that I'm not spending precious hours in a cloud of smoke. Am I using my time to good advantage?

Day 80

"I had to stop smoking before I could quit."

None of us have had identical experiences with quitting tobacco. It's valuable to acknowledge there are no right or wrong ways to achieve our goal. It's equally valuable to understand we can learn from one another's experiences.

Sharing our stories about what it was like for us and how and why we quit is a way of helping ourselves stay committed to this undertaking; it's also a way of showing support for someone who's trying to make the decision to take the plunge. It's particularly good for us in this third month of our abstinence to strengthen our personal gratitude for the changes that have occurred since we stopped. Sharing our story guarantees another measure of gratitude.

For some, there's a subtle but important difference between stopping smoking and quitting. Others reprogram themselves to be "born anew" as nonsmokers. The manner of our stopping isn't important. That we do stop is paramount.

**An opportunity will come today to tell someone else
about my smoking past. I'll take it!**

Day 81

---

*"I liked going out in the woods to hike, but I realized
I couldn't. I needed to be near a drugstore."*

Nicotine made prisoners of us. It determined where we could comfortably go and how long we could stay. It demanded our time, attention, money, and a ready supply. We shamelessly sorted through coat pockets, trash, and dirty ashtrays in search of smokeable butts and left children unattended late at night while we rushed to the store for another pack. What a relief to be leaving those days behind.

Nicotine's power is subtle, baffling, and consuming. Until we're very comfortably settled as nonsmokers, we must be vigilant about our behavior around cigarettes. Urges will tempt us, but one cigarette will never be enough.

It's very important in these early months of not smoking to explore new activities and develop new interests. We must refocus our energies in fulfilling ways to reap some meaningful benefits from not smoking—as quickly as possible. Old habits die hard unless new ones take their place.

I'll be open to working on a healthy habit today.

Day 82

"At frequent intervals, I imaged myself as a smiling, confident nonsmoker."

For people from all walks of life and for thousands of reasons, visualization is a technique that has been used successfully—by athletes preparing for intense sporting events, actors before a performance, and speakers before an important speech. Visualization is a creative form of self-teaching. In our minds, we practice our stance or our delivery for when the hour of the real performance beckons.

It's not immediate that we think of ourselves as nonsmokers; it's sensible to help the process along in whatever ways are possible. The use of imagery is simple, successful if practiced, and easily accessible; it can be done in a flash and in any setting—a crowded bus, a busy restaurant, or the quiet of an office or study. We close our eyes and draw our picture—carefully and in detail. We dwell on it, savor it for a moment, and then go on about life.

Our belief in ourselves as nonsmokers will be hastened and strengthened through the power of imagery.

Today I'll use my mind to strengthen my new identity as a nonsmoker as often as possible.

Day 83

"It's so much more comfortable being a nonsmoker. There are so many places where smoking is discouraged—if not flatly prohibited."

I hated the negative attention I attracted because of my smoking. I feared asking for a table in a restaurant smoking section when I was dining with nonsmoking friends. But I feared even more sitting through an entire meal, waiting through all the conversation without a cigarette. I feared parties in homes where the hosts didn't smoke or vape. I thought I needed to smoke to think, to talk, or to listen to others. Now I know my need to smoke was my own subtle escape from myself and the situation.

The feeling of no longer being imprisoned by the demands of my nicotine habit is like being born again. The freedom we now have can empower us to explore new territories, new activities, new ideas. No longer must we deny ourselves an experience because we have to go and satisfy a tobacco craving. Our decision to give up nicotine has set us free to fulfill our pride and our goals.

I pray for the willingness to be grateful for my freedom today. It is paving the way for me to grow and change in terribly important ways.

Day 84

"One of the keys to successfully quitting was I had to stop lying to myself about what cigarettes did and did not do for me."

Cigarettes really didn't make us sophisticated, even though it seemed that way. nor did they help us solve problems or make us more articulate or creative. And they certainly didn't improve our well-being. However, our delusion convinced us that they did all these things and more.

Tobacco's power was cunning and baffling. It made our decisions for us. It chose our direction and defined our goals and limitations, and it waits in the wings to take charge of us again.

Let's rejoice that we've come this far. Gratitude for our many days as nonsmokers will strengthen us. We've solved many problems without the consolation of a cigarette. We've conversed and been understood; and we've managed many tasks that we had mistakenly feared could only be accomplished with the help of a cigarette.

How wrong I was, thinking I needed a cigarette to achieve a goal. I'm free! What an exhilarating realization.

Day 85

"Even now, after ten years, if I were to have one,
I know I'd start smoking again."

I need to be forever vigilant when I encounter the urge for a single cigarette, or even a single puff. For us nicotine addicts, there is no such thing as "just one." Many of us have had to learn and relearn that lesson many times in the past. Let's not make ourselves have to relearn it again today.

Being glad I don't smoke while still wanting just one more is not an unusual circumstance. To get me through a momentary longing, I quietly pray I can remember the benefits that accompany the choice I've made to be free from this habit. I am healthier. I do smell better. And I have more time freed up for friends, personal goals, and fun.

I'll be in charge of my life today.
I'll not give my power over to nicotine.

Day 86

---

*"I'm willing to go through pain if there's a benefit,
but with smoking there's no benefit."*

It's only because of our delusion that we thought smoking benefited our lives. Certainly, when we started smoking, most of us assumed it made us appear sophisticated, or at least grown-up. At the time, that seemed like a benefit.

Tobacco has turned on us just as other drugs do in time. Coughing, colds, chest pains, shortness of breath, stained teeth and fingers; we've experienced all of these during our years of use. But what were the benefits?

It's painful to adjust to life's many turmoils with a mind that's attentive and clear, not focused on the next cigarette. In reality, nicotine has allowed us to escape great leaps of growth we had earned through experience by muffling the feelings that would have spurred our forward movements.

**As a nonsmoker, I'm giving myself opportunities to grow,
opportunities that may not come around again.**

Day 87

---

*"I'm less edgy and less frustrated,
and I'm more effective as a nonsmoker."*

Choosing not to smoke is giving me a sense of personal power that I didn't have before. I can make decisions that benefit me! I am in control of my actions and my attitudes.

For a long time, I didn't really want to smoke, but I did anyway. I felt ashamed, sometimes angry, and preoccupied with it. My preoccupation often took my attention away from people and activities I really cared about. It's easier now to be organized with my life. I no longer keep interrupting my chain of thought to search for cigarettes, lighter, or vape pen. The events of the day flow more smoothly. I'm not in need of the perpetual "break" to satisfy a craving for nicotine. Being a nonsmoker has added a rich dimension to the fabric of my life.

**I know I think better, look better, and smell better as a
nonsmoker, and the decision to be one is solely mine, today.**

Day 88

---

*"I've learned through all of my false starts that coming
to terms with being a nonsmoker is really coming to
terms with taking responsibility for my health,
as well as changing my inner picture of who I am."*

I am personally responsible for who I am, how I behave, what I think, how I feel, and who I become. My attitudes about other people, each situation that arises, and myself are solely manufactured in the confines of my mind. And I will be as happy each day as I make up my mind to be—about work, relationships, not smoking, and other personal achievements.

Sensing our personal power is exhilarating. Knowing we're in control of the decision to smoke or not smoke, vape or not vape, nurtures the inner self. Acting responsibly in the face of all the evidence about the harmful effects of nicotine is like heaping praises on the soul. It's affirming to know we're worthy of life.

**My self-respect is heightened each day I choose not
to smoke. Both my inner self and my physical body are
realizing greater health, too.**

Day 89

"The best thing about not smoking is being free
of the control it had over me."

Cigarettes used to control my every action. Before meals, after meals, while driving, talking on the phone, or relaxing, cigarettes were a necessity. What a surprise to discover I can go about my daily activities without relying on tobacco for companionship or comfort. I can make decisions without a cigarette, and I can go from home to work or out to visit a friend without having to check on my supply.

Most of us didn't realize we were prisoners of our nicotine habit, at least not until we had decided to quit. Then it became so very clear. Few of us would ever have allowed another person the amount of control over us that we so willingly relinquished to nicotine. How glad we can be that habitual surrender is a thing of the past.

I am my own person now, and I love the challenge of my decisions and the strength bestowed on me as a result.

Day 90

---

*"It seems all of us are given the choice to make
the best of our opportunities. Some of us will."*

Hindsight so clearly details which opportunities we've taken up and which ones we've missed. Our progress to date in our work and in our personal lives is a clear indication of our responses to opportunities. Let's be aware that each moment is rich with opportunity, now as in the past. Our openness and attention to these moments clearly determines how far we'll go.

Presently, through reading these lines, we're taking advantage of an opportunity to support our own decision to give up tobacco. For none of us has it been an easy decision every day; but we've made it, and now it's month three.

Many of us have quit before, but our resolve and our willingness are greater this time. We're not struggling alone this time. We're open to the help available from others, from these words, and from the Spirit within. We can be grateful that we've responded well to an opportunity to quit with others rather than in isolation.

**I'm not alone. All around people are becoming nonsmokers.
I'll say a small prayer for all of us.**

Afterword

There's nothing to prevent you from going back to day one and reading once again the messages that most speak to you—the new nonsmoker. Most of us continue to need support and comfort; a second reading of all or some of the meditations will offer strength as well as solace.

Many people throughout the world rely on the ongoing support that daily meditations provide. Those of us in search of continuing personal growth realize that we're always "becoming"—that the adventure never ends. And we specifically discover that the growth we attain allows us to see anew the many subtle meanings inherent in each page of every meditation book. The more we grow, the more we can see possibilities for even further growth.

So do not feel that the advice, stories, and meditations provided here can offer you nothing more. Their job has perhaps only just begun. Treat these messages as friends who will never abandon you, but who will comfort you in the days and months ahead.

Acknowledgments

———————

I learned so much from writing this book. In its own way, each story I listened to helped me better understand my own personal commitment to being a nonsmoker. I deeply thank each of the people who took the time to talk with me. It's my hope that I've conveyed their stories accurately, without distortion, and with a sense of their love for all who want to join our ranks as nonsmokers.

I especially want to thank my husband Joe for exploring with me the direction this book should take. Initially I was off course, and he risked sharing his perception, and in the process, guided me to the book's present form. His instincts were wonderful and on target. I loved our collaboration.

And I want to thank you, the reader, for daring to risk living life free of tobacco. The road will feel long and lonely at times, but there are millions of us who have gone before, and our spirits are traveling with you. As our numbers multiply, our environment grows safer for all humanity. Future generations will reap many blessings from our courageous decision. Peace be with you.

About the Author

K aren Casey, winner of a 2007 Johnson Institute America Honors Recovery Award for her contributions to the field, is a sought-after speaker at recovery and spirituality conferences throughout the country. She has written thirty-one books, among them *Each Day a Renewed Beginning: Meditations for a Peaceful Journey, Peace a Day at a Time, 52 Ways to Live the Course in Miracles, 20 Things I Know for Sure, It's Up to You, Codependence and the Power of Detachment*, and *Change Your Mind and Your Life Will Follow*—a bestselling book that is the basis for her Change Your Mind Workshops—plus many more. This daily meditation book you are now holding was originally published in 1982, has sold more than four million copies, and has been translated into ten different languages. To learn more about her work, visit her at www.womens-spirituality.com or her Facebook page: Karen Casey, Author.

Mango Publishing, established in 2014, publishes an eclectic list of books by diverse authors—both new and established voices—on topics ranging from business, personal growth, women's empowerment, LGBTQ studies, health, and spirituality to history, popular culture, time management, decluttering, lifestyle, mental wellness, aging, and sustainable living. We were named 2019 *and* 2020's #1 fastest growing independent publisher by *Publishers Weekly*. Our success is driven by our main goal, which is to publish high-quality books that will entertain readers as well as make a positive difference in their lives.

Our readers are our most important resource; we value your input, suggestions, and ideas. We'd love to hear from you—after all, we are publishing books for you!

Please stay in touch with us and follow us at:

Facebook: Mango Publishing

Twitter: @MangoPublishing

Instagram: @MangoPublishing

LinkedIn: Mango Publishing

Pinterest: Mango Publishing

Newsletter: mangopublishinggroup.com/newsletter

Join us on Mango's journey to reinvent publishing, one book at a time.

9 781684 814848